VINITA HA

2025

A Book of
Grace-Filled
Days

LOYOLAPRESS.
A JESUIT MINISTRY

Chicago

LOYOLA PRESS.
A JESUIT MINISTRY

www.loyolapress.com

Cover and interior design by Kathy Kikkert.

ISBN: 978-0-8294-5630-1

Printed in the United States of America.
24 25 26 27 28 29 30 31 32 33 Versa 10 9 8 7 6 5 4 3 2 1

INTRODUCTION

The Christian Scriptures are living documents. What I mean is, they continue to bear fruit, to give us life, to offer wisdom. For millennia, they have instructed, comforted, strengthened, and formed the lives of those who turned to them, believing these words to be inspired, generated from the very presence of God.

Yet, it's no simple thing to read, interpret, and live out what we find in the Bible. Our Christian Scriptures are a complex patchwork of stories, instructions, poetry, and other sorts of literature. Saints of great learning and holiness have wrestled with this patchwork. As much as we'd like to think there's a "right" way to read a passage, the truth is, even the saints haven't agreed at times on what is meant by a certain parable of Jesus or a phrase used by St. Paul or St. Luke.

How, then, is an individual like you or me to approach God's word? Do we need a degree in theology? Can we trust ourselves to understand what is there for us in the story or the proverb?

We can trust the Holy Spirit, whose work is to help us learn and remember. We can trust Jesus, who walks alongside us. We can also trust the word itself to delve into our minds and hearts and reveal to us what a phrase or verse might illuminate this day. And we can trust our own humble, open hearts. God honors the seeker. God communicates to the hungry soul. Let us proceed, then, through this year, with faith in the Father, Son, and Holy Spirit to accompany us as we sit with the Scriptures and allow them to do their life-giving work in us, one graced day after another.

[Jesus said to his disciples,]
"There will be signs in the sun, the moon, and the stars,
and on earth nations will be in dismay,
perplexed by the roaring of the sea and the waves."
—LUKE 21:25

These are not happy words for beginning Advent, but now is
a good time to remember that Jesus came not only as savior
but as prophet. He told us what we needed to hear. He still
does, if we let go of our need for happiness and perpetual
sunshine and listen to him. While we await the sweet babe in
the manger, can we also anticipate the Incarnate One who
comes to transform us?

Jeremiah 33:14–16
Psalm 25:4–5,8–9,10,14 (1b)
1 Thessalonians 3:12—4:2
Luke 21:25–28,34–36

⋺ 1 ⋲

I rejoiced because they said to me,
"We will go up to the house of the LORD."
—PSALM 122:1

We move toward a new way of being, a way in which our security, our hope, our purpose—our everything—thrives in the reality we call God. God's very presence, God's glory, will shelter, protect, and comfort us. Try not to think of God's house as a physical building; not all worship spaces are majestic or beautiful or welcoming. Instead, imagine a space infused with the eternal, powerful, loving presence of God.

Isaiah 2:1–5
Psalm 122:1–2,3–4b,4cd–5,6–7,8–9
Matthew 8:5–11

[Jesus said,] "For I say to you,
many prophets and kings desired to see what you see,
but did not see it,
and to hear what you hear, but did not hear it."
—LUKE 10:24

Although during Advent we might anticipate food, gifts, and festivities to come at Christmas, how easily we forget the tremendous importance of the Child we have been given. We know what many before us longed to hear about him. We have the story of Jesus, the Christ. Others had only shadowy beginnings of the story, yet they hoped and waited. May we honor our waiting with wonder.

Isaiah 11:1–10
Psalm 72:1–2,7–8,12–13,17
Luke 10:21–24

Wednesday

DECEMBER 4

• ST. JOHN DAMASCENE, PRIEST AND DOCTOR OF THE CHURCH •

On this mountain [the LORD] will destroy
the veil that veils all peoples,
the web that is woven over all nations;
he will destroy death forever.
—ISAIAH 25:7–8A

Do we comprehend how veiled we are from the truth and holiness of God? No matter how hard we try to live a holy life, there is always some distance, like a partition, between God and us. During this season of hope, we anticipate the coming year during which we pray to have less and less standing between us and our heavenly Father. We anticipate the growth of our intimacy with the divine.

Isaiah 25:6–10a
Psalm 23:1–3a,3b–4,5,6
Matthew 15:29–37

⇒ 4 ⇐

DECEMBER 5

Open to me the gates of justice;
I will enter them and give thanks to the LORD.
—PSALM 118:19

Jesus comes to bring us justice, among other things. We wait
and wait for justice, don't we? Watching the poor suffer, the
marginalized get erased from public consciousness, the
egotistical and power-hungry throwing their weight around
and causing damage—through the millennia, people have
waited for the world to be put right. We can continue our
prayers and efforts toward justice, and Advent is certainly an
appropriate season for that.

Isaiah 26:1–6
Psalm 118:1 and 8–9,19–21,25–27a
Matthew 7:21,24–27

Those who err in spirit shall acquire understanding,
and those who find fault shall receive instruction.
—ISAIAH 29:24

When I was learning to knit, I looked and waited for someone who could instruct me. I was trying hard and doing my best, but I needed help. I also need help in learning to live as a beloved child of God. Jesus' coming to live among us provided the instruction we so desperately needed. That alone is worth a few weeks of Advent hope!

Isaiah 29:17–24
Psalm 27:1,4,13–14
Matthew 9:27–31

Saturday

DECEMBER 7

• ST. AMBROSE, BISHOP AND DOCTOR OF THE CHURCH •

*The Lord will give you the bread you need
and the water for which you thirst.*
—ISAIAH 30:20

Having lived through the COVID-19 pandemic of 2020–2022, I have more appreciation for having access to food and water. When supply chains of all sorts developed problems or broke down altogether, I was reminded that, ultimately, all I receive comes from the same loving Creator who made the world and all its riches. Jesus called himself the bread of life and the water of life. He came to supply the satisfaction for which every person longs—the kind of food and drink the soul longs for.

Isaiah 30:19–21,23–26
Psalm 147:1–2,3–4,5–6
Matthew 9:35—10:1,5a,6–8

DECEMBER 8

• SECOND SUNDAY OF ADVENT •

And this is my prayer:
that your love may increase ever more and more
in knowledge and every kind of perception,
to discern what is of value,
so that you may be pure and blameless for the day of Christ,
filled with the fruit of righteousness
that comes through Jesus Christ
for the glory and praise of God.
—PHILIPPIANS 1:9–11

Pray this prayer for yourself today, and for your loved ones,
and for your faith community, for the whole world in fact.
A prayer of holiness and hope.

Baruch 5:1–9
Psalm 126:1–2,2,2–3,4–5,6 (3)
Philippians 1:4–6,8–11
Luke 3:1–6

DECEMBER 9

I will put enmity between you and the woman,
and between your offspring and hers;
he will strike at your head,
while you strike at his heel.
—GENESIS 3:15

Mary became a primary instrument in the defeat of the evil one. Her son struck the serpent's head, but Mary bore the son, brought him up, and taught him. Little wonder we offer her such enduring honor.

Genesis 3:9–15,20
Psalm 98:1,2–3ab,3cd–4
Ephesians 1:3–6,11–12
Luke 1:26–38

DECEMBER 10

[Jesus said to his disciples,]
"What is your opinion?
If a man has a hundred sheep and one of them goes astray,
will he not leave the ninety-nine in the hills
and go in search of the stray?
—MATTHEW 18:12

God seeks us to bring us home as a shepherd goes looking
for the one lost sheep. May our desire to be found grow
more and more during this Advent season. Do we want to be
found? Do we truly want to find our home in God?

Isaiah 40:1–11
Psalm 96:1–2,3 and 10ac,11–12,13
Matthew 18:12–14

[Jesus said to the crowds,]
"Come to me, all you who labor and are burdened,
and I will give you rest."
—MATTHEW 11:28

Our assumption is that a burdened person wants relief and that someone hard at work wants to rest. But is that always true? The person who maintains her identity from working seventy-hour weeks may not be so willing to stop. The man whose sense of purpose comes from his many burdens may resist giving up any of them. While we "wait" for God to help us, it is wise for us to assess what we truly want, what we are willing to give up, and what help we are willing to receive.

Isaiah 40:25–31
Psalm 103:1–2,3–4,8 and 10
Matthew 11:28–30

DECEMBER 12

• OUR LADY OF GUADALUPE •

Many nations shall join themselves to the LORD on that day,
and they shall be his people,
and he will dwell among you,
and you shall know that the LORD of hosts has sent me to you.
—ZECHARIAH 2:15

Zechariah could not have imagined just how many nations would be welcomed into God's domain and how far-flung those nations would be. Our Lady of Guadalupe sojourned the realms to reach a poor man in Mexico and thus bring faith and hope to an entire people. Where else might she show up? What brothers and sisters have we yet to meet?

Zechariah 2:14–17 or Revelation 11:19a; 12:1–6a,10ab
Judith 13:18bcde,19
Luke 1:26–38 or 1:39–47
Or any readings from the Common of the Blessed Virgin Mary

DECEMBER 13

• ST. LUCY, VIRGIN AND MARTYR •

I, the LORD, your God,
teach you what is for your good,
and lead you on the way you should go.
—ISAIAH 48:17

We can follow a leader yet not know where that leader is
taking us. Thus, Advent anticipation can be edged with
apprehension: How will Jesus appear to me this time? What
doors will God ask me to walk through? God is trustworthy,
and I believe that God loves me. And so I continue to follow,
even as I walk into the unknown.

Isaiah 48:17–19
Psalm 1:1–2,3,4 and 6
Matthew 11:16–19

Saturday

DECEMBER 14

• ST. JOHN OF THE CROSS, PRIEST AND DOCTOR OF THE CHURCH •

[Jesus said,] "Elijah will indeed come and restore all things;
but I tell you that Elijah has already come,
and they did not recognize him but did to him whatever they pleased. . . .
Then the disciples understood
that he was speaking to them of John the Baptist.
—MATTHEW 17:11–13

We like to look ahead, but sometimes God asks us to look
back and see a person, event, or situation in a different light.
Are there people in your life who deserve a second look,
people God may have placed there for a specific reason that
you didn't see at the time? It's worth some prayer and
reflection.

Sirach 48:1–4,9–11
Psalm 80:2ac and 3b,15–16,18–19
Matthew 17:9a,10–13

Sunday

DECEMBER 15

• THIRD SUNDAY OF ADVENT •

*The crowds asked John the Baptist,
"What should we do?"
He said to them in reply,
"Whoever has two cloaks
should share with the person who has none.
And whoever has food should do likewise."*
—LUKE 3:10–11

The people were asking a foundational question of possibly the most holy and charismatic person they had ever met, a man with God's Spirit upon him. Sort of like one of us getting the opportunity to ask Pope Francis our one most important question. And the answer was embarrassingly simple: do what you can to help the people right in front of you. God's call upon us is rarely complicated, but it is challenging, isn't it?

Zephaniah 3:14–18a
Isaiah 12:2–3,4,5–6 (6)
Philippians 4:4–7
Luke 3:10–18

DECEMBER 16

> *[Balaam said,] "I see him, though not now;*
> *I behold him, though not near:*
> *A star shall advance from Jacob,*
> *and a staff shall rise from Israel."*
> —NUMBERS 24:17

The ancients had such a deep and expansive view of history, didn't they? A prophet knew that he or she perhaps saw ahead hundreds of years; yet the prophecy, the Good News, brought great joy in the present. People of today are ridiculously impatient, looking for short-term and immediate results and allowing deeper visions and more important goals to dissipate and lose their meaning. Let's be daring and invite those expansive visions. Let's allow our hope and joy to anticipate the Good News in generations beyond us.

Numbers 24:2–7,15–17a
Psalm 25:4–5ab,6 and 7bc,8–9
Matthew 21:23–27

Tuesday

DECEMBER 17

*Justice shall flower in his days,
and profound peace, till the moon be no more.
May he rule from sea to sea,
and from the River to the ends of the earth.*
—PSALM 72:7–8

These words describe the rule of a good king. This psalm is a prayer about the king of God's people. Thousands of years later, we naturally think of this king as Jesus, who is ultimate King over all creation. We look forward to every characteristic of his rule coming to pass. We can also, however, pray that, during the limited days of earthly leaders—presidents, prime ministers, ambassadors—the qualities of holy leadership will manifest. May we not grow weary in these prayers.

Genesis 49:2,8–10
Psalm 72:1–2,3–4ab,7–8,17
Matthew 1:1–17

DECEMBER 18

When Joseph awoke,
he did as the angel of the Lord had commanded him
and took his wife into his home.
—MATTHEW 1:24

What a simple sentence, but it describes a reality that was not at all simple. Joseph's betrothed was in fact already pregnant, and not by Joseph. When Joseph followed God's instructions as given to him in a dream, he took on a difficult life. First of all, others likely knew that Mary was pregnant: she returned from her visit with cousin Elizabeth after three months, and a three-month pregnancy shows on a young girl. We have no way of knowing how hard the couple's life was in their small, close-knit community after that. Joseph did a simple thing: he took his betrothed into his home. But this was no easy choice. Indeed, this first choice foreshadowed a life of various dreams and dangers to come.

Jeremiah 23:5–8
Psalm 72:1–2,12–13,18–19
Matthew 1:18–25

DECEMBER 19

[The angel Gabriel said,]
"But now you will be speechless and unable to talk
until the day these things take place,
because you did not believe my words,
which will be fulfilled at their proper time."
—LUKE 1:20

Mary asked Gabriel how it was possible to have a child when
she had not been with a man, and Gabriel gave her an
explanation. Zechariah, an elderly and righteous priest,
questioned how he and his wife could possibly have a baby,
and Gabriel responded with anger. Was it because, given
Zechariah's long history with God, he should have known
better? Or can even an established believer and longtime
follower of God grow weary, disillusioned, full of doubts,
even cynical? We don't know Zechariah's heart, but it's clear
that age, reputation, wisdom, and position cannot compete
with simple faith in a young and open heart.

Judges 13:2–7,24–25a
Psalm 71:3–4a,5–6ab,16–17
Luke 1:5–25

The LORD spoke to Ahaz:
Ask for a sign from the LORD, your God;
let it be deep as the nether world, or high as the sky!
But Ahaz answered,
"I will not ask! I will not tempt the LORD!" . . .
Therefore the Lord himself will give you this sign:
the virgin shall conceive and bear a son,
and shall name him Emmanuel.
—ISAIAH 7:10–14

God offered to give Ahaz any sign he wanted, but Ahaz shrank from this invitation. What would he think now, to understand that his unwillingness to engage with God resulted in what we know as the great Incarnation! Let's not be shy with God of the Universe.

Isaiah 7:10–14
Psalm 24:1–2,3–4ab,5–6
Luke 1:26–38

Saturday

DECEMBER 21

· ST. PETER CANISIUS, PRIEST AND DOCTOR OF THE CHURCH ·

The LORD, your God, is in your midst,
a mighty savior;
He will rejoice over you with gladness,
and renew you in his love,
He will sing joyfully because of you,
as one sings at festivals.
—ZEPHANIAH 3:17–18A

During Advent, we look forward to the coming of God into
our midst. Let's stop and ponder this: God *looked forward* to
the Incarnation. God anticipated being among us, loving us,
rejoicing over us. Let that sink in today.

Song of Songs 2:8–14 or Zephaniah 3:14–18a
Psalm 33:2–3,11–12,20–21
Luke 1:39–45

⇒ 21 ⇐

DECEMBER 22

• FOURTH SUNDAY OF ADVENT •

*He shall stand firm and shepherd his flock
by the strength of the LORD, . . .
for now his greatness
shall reach to the ends of the earth;
he shall be peace.*
—MICAH 5:3–4A

Jesus would be born in a certain place, to a certain family, at a certain time. But that was just the beginning. He would take on the role of shepherd for the human race, extending his love and power throughout the world. While we focus on the Christmas season with all its traditions and food and family endeavors, may we not lose sight of God's ultimate purpose in Jesus: to be our universal peace.

Micah 5:1–4a
Psalm 80:2–3,15–16,18–19 (4)
Hebrews 10:5–10
Luke 1:39–45

Yes, he is coming, says the LORD of hosts.
And who can stand when he appears?
For he is like the refiner's fire.
—MALACHI 3:1B–2

How often have I sung a hymn in church, asking the Holy Spirit to "come," "fall afresh on me," "fill this place"? As if I am truly ready for the Holy Spirit to do a mighty work in my life! As if God's work in me is some easy, happy thing. For centuries, God's people looked for and asked for their Messiah. But when he arrived, they were unpleasantly surprised. He required that they sort out their lives, get rid of unholy attachments, love God and neighbor, give up their idols. As we await the Christ child, we would be wise to prepare our hearts, not for the warm glow of a Nativity scene, but for the shock of inner revolution.

Malachi 3:1–4,23–24
Psalm 25:4–5ab,8–9,10 and 14
Luke 1:57–66

In the tender compassion of our God
the dawn from on high shall break upon us,
to shine on those who dwell in darkness and the shadow of death,
and to guide our feet into the way of peace.
—LUKE 1:78–79

I have memorized this bit of Zechariah's great song. I murmur these words to remind myself of what God has already done. I recite this verse to remember that Jesus the Christ came for those in the shadows of struggle, pain, and death. I pray this verse to recall that I must always be walking toward peace.

2 Samuel 7:1–5,8b–12,14a,16
Psalm 89:2–3,4–5,27 and 29
Luke 1:67–79

Wednesday

DECEMBER 25

• THE NATIVITY OF THE LORD (CHRISTMAS) •

From his fullness we have all received,
grace in place of grace,
because while the law was given through Moses,
grace and truth came through Jesus Christ.

—JOHN 1:16–17

A mighty shift has occurred in the universe: grace and truth
have come to us in a person, whose name is Jesus, or
Emmanuel: "God with Us." We can only respond with relief,
thanksgiving, and joy.

VIGIL:
Isaiah 62:1–5
Psalm 89:4–5,16–17,27,29 (2a)
Acts 13:16–17,22–25
Matthew 1:1–25 or 1:18–25

NIGHT:
Isaiah 9:1–6
Psalm 96:1–2,2–3,11–12,13
Titus 2:11–14
Luke 2:1–14

DAWN:
Isaiah 62:11–12
Psalm 97:1,6,11–12
Titus 3:4–7
Luke 2:15–20

DAY:
Isaiah 52:7–10
Psalm 98:1,2–3,3–4,5–6 (3c)
Hebrews 1:1–6
John 1:1–18 or 1:1–5,9–14

Thursday

DECEMBER 26

• ST. STEPHEN, THE FIRST MARTYR •

*"Brother will hand over brother to death,
and the father his child;
children will rise up against parents and have them put to death."*
—MATTHEW 10:21

In this world deep deposits of antipathy run against the way of love. We derive satisfaction from hatred and vengeance. It pleases ego and pride to win an argument. And power is addictive. Jesus knew that the way of love, justice, and peace would provoke horrible reactions, even within families. Thus, we should not be surprised at the painful rifts that occur simply because we choose to follow Jesus. Jesus warned us about this long ago. He asks that we trust him and endure.

Acts 6:8–10; 7:54–59
Psalm 31:3cd–4,6 and 8ab,16bc and 17
Matthew 10:17–22

⇒ 26 ⇐

Light dawns for the just;
and gladness, for the upright of heart.
Be glad in the LORD, you just,
and give thanks to his holy name.
—PSALM 97:11–12

Jesus' resurrection brought joy to those who desired God's kingdom here on earth as well as in heaven. If we long for the world Jesus longs for, his birth, life, death, and resurrection are sources of joy and hope. Jesus will always be moving toward justice, peace, restoration, compassion, and joy. We can ask this day, "Am I moving toward those things? Do I find joy in what gives Jesus joy?"

1 John 1:1–4
Psalm 97:1–2,5–6,11–12
John 20:1a and 2–8

If we say, "We are without sin,"
we deceive ourselves, and the truth is not in us.
If we acknowledge our sins, he is faithful and just
and will forgive our sins and cleanse us from every wrongdoing.
—1 JOHN 1:8–9

It's tempting to take this passage in a simplistic way: *If I do this, then God will do that. I just need to admit my sins, and then I'll be good with God.* But what is at the heart of this passage? Honesty. I can claim innocence, but that would simply be a lie. When I'm dishonest with myself and others, I can't make any spiritual progress. But once I'm honest with God, then God can work with me, can heal and restore me. This is not about saying what God wants to hear but about speaking the truth always, especially when the truth is hard to admit.

1 John 1:5—2:2
Psalm 124:2–3,4–5,7b–8
Matthew 2:13–18

DECEMBER 29

"I prayed for this child, and the LORD granted my request.
Now I, in turn, give him to the LORD;
as long as he lives, he shall be dedicated to the LORD."
Hannah left Samuel there.
—1 SAMUEL 1:27–28

Here's a woman who, barren for years, begged God for a child. When God gave her a son, she gave the son right back to God after the boy was weaned, according to a vow she had made. Her most precious gift from God is the very child she gives back to God. After all those years of longing, now she must be without her boy before he's even school age. She kept her vow. But perhaps she recognized that the child—any child—is already the Lord's. Can we think of our children as God's and not ours? What kind of shift in attitude must happen?

1 Samuel 1:20–22,24–28
Psalm 84:2–3,5–6,9–10
1 John 3:1–2,21–24
Luke 2:41–52
Or, in Year A, Sirach 3:2–6,12–14 / Colossians 3:12–21 / Luke 2:41–52

DECEMBER 30

*And coming forward at that very time,
[Anna] gave thanks to God and spoke about the child
to all who were awaiting the redemption of Jerusalem.*
—LUKE 2:38

Anna had spent a long life in the temple, praying and
fasting—until a certain day when a couple brought their
baby boy to the temple and the old woman understood that
she had been waiting for this day all along. Her many years
of prayer, of dwelling in God's presence, now made her
sensitive to a phenomenal truth: this child would redeem
God's people. When we spend years learning to pray and sit
with our Lord, we don't know what we may see and
understand one day. But that closeness to God can bring
extraordinary wisdom and intuition.
It's for us to pay attention.

1 John 2:12–17
Psalm 96:7–8a,8b–9,10
Luke 2:36–40

DECEMBER 31

• ST. SYLVESTER I, POPE •

What came to be through him was life,
and this life was the light of the human race;
the light shines in the darkness,
and the darkness has not overcome it.

—JOHN 1:4–5

We have come to the end of another year, and we can testify that the light of Christ continues to shine. There's much darkness in the world, but still we are given this light; it shines through our very humanity. It breaks through our ordinary days and nights and helps us to see and understand, to work and flourish. May we look ahead to the new year, encouraged by this enduring, warming light.

1 John 2:18–21
Psalm 96:1–2,11–12,13
John 1:1–18

Wednesday

JANUARY 1

Say to them:
The LORD bless you and keep you!
The LORD let his face shine upon you, and be gracious to you!
The LORD look upon you kindly and give you peace!
—NUMBERS 6:23–26

What a beautiful prayer for the first day of the year! This is a blessing God gave to Moses to give to Aaron, the words he and his sons could use to bless the Israelites. In other words, it's a good all-around blessing, one we can speak to one another, one we can pray for anyone. It's just as holy and hopeful now as it was way back then.

Numbers 6:22–27
Psalm 67:2–3,5,6,8 (2a)
Galatians 4:4–7
Luke 2:16–21

JANUARY 2

• ST. BASIL THE GREAT AND ST. GREGORY NAZIANZEN,
BISHOPS AND DOCTORS OF THE CHURCH •

Sing to the LORD a new song,
for he has done wondrous deeds. . . .
All the ends of the earth have seen
the salvation by our God.
Sing joyfully to the LORD, all you lands;
break into song; sing praise.
—PSALM 98:1–2

We enter a new year remembering all that God has done;
perhaps we review how God was present to us during the
previous year. We begin the year with joy because we know
our God is loving, merciful, wise, and powerful. We start out
the new year with praise, not with anxiety; with gratitude,
not with dread.

1 John 2:22–28
Psalm 98:1,2–3ab,3cd–4
John 1:19–28

[John the Baptist said,] "I did not know him,
but the reason why I came baptizing with water
was that he might be made known to Israel . . .
On whomever you see the Spirit come down and remain,
he is the one who will baptize with the Holy Spirit."
—JOHN 1:31–32

Even John did not know who would be the Messiah, though
he undoubtedly knew Jesus. They were related, and their
mothers had formed a strong bond when Mary stayed with
Elizabeth prior to John's birth. The two women knew that
their sons had extraordinary callings, and perhaps they had
mentioned, carefully, some of this information while the boys
were growing up. But John waited for the Spirit to make clear
to him that Jesus was the one for whom John had prepared
the people. May we put aside our opinions and speculations
and faithfully wait for the Spirit's leading.

1 John 2:29—3:6
Psalm 98:1,3cd–4,5–6
John 1:29–34

Saturday

JANUARY 4

• ST. ELIZABETH ANN SETON, RELIGIOUS •

Jesus turned and saw them following him and said to them,
"What are you looking for?"
They said to him, "Rabbi" (which translated means Teacher),
"where are you staying?"
He said to them, "Come, and you will see."
—JOHN 1:38–39

Jesus could have simply told these men where he was staying,
but he used their question as an opportunity to invite them
along. Nothing beats hanging out with a person. Jesus knew
that these men would either be drawn to his works and
message or they would quickly lose interest. They were free
to come and see, and then choose what they would do.
Perhaps we spend too much time and energy trying to
explain our faith to people when, really, we should just invite
them to join us as we go about the work of God's kingdom.

1 John 3:7–10
Psalm 98:1,7–8,9
John 1:35–42

Sunday

JANUARY 5

• THE EPIPHANY OF THE LORD •

They were overjoyed at seeing the star,
and on entering the house
they saw the child with Mary his mother.
—MATTHEW 2:10–11

According to earlychurchhistory.org, "In the ancient Middle Eastern world these Magi were trusted advisors to kings, were learned men proficient in the knowledge of mathematical calculations, astronomy, medicine, astrology, alchemy, dream interpretation and history as well as practitioners of magic and paranormal arts." And yet, their professional curiosity, knowledge, and skill brought them to a child and his mother. The greatest mysteries are contained within us: humans made in the divine image.

Isaiah 60:1–6
Psalm 72:1–2,7–8,10–11,12–13
Ephesians 3:2–3a,5–6
Matthew 2:1–12

JANUARY 6

Those who keep his commandments remain in him, and he in them,
and the way we know that he remains in us
is from the Spirit whom he gave us.
—1 JOHN 3:24

A person of immature faith worries about not breaking God's rules and about obeying God's commands. But as we grow in our friendship with God, we focus more and more on staying in harmony with what God is doing in the world. In other words, we don't fear punishment as much as we desire to collaborate with Jesus and participate in his work. This is made possible by the Holy Spirit dwelling within us, helping us to follow Jesus' example, and reminding us of what we have learned.

1 John 3:22—4:6
Psalm 2:7bc–8,10–12a
Matthew 4:12–17,23–25

JANUARY 7

• ST. RAYMOND OF PENYAFORT, PRIEST •

O God, with your judgment endow the king,
and with your justice, the king's son;
He shall govern your people with justice
and your afflicted ones with judgment.

—PSALM 72:2

These words make an appropriate prayer for anyone in a
position of leadership and power. Ask God to endow leaders
with justice, good sense, mercy, and compassion. We can
trust that God is always inviting the powerful to be
transformed, to do in this world what is right and good.

1 John 4:7–10
Psalm 72:1–2,3–4,7–8
Mark 6:34–44

JANUARY 8

God is love,
and whoever remains in love remains in God and God in him.
In this is love brought to perfection among us,
that we have confidence on the day of judgment
because as he is, so are we in this world.

—1 JOHN 4:16–17

God's great desire, and Jesus' overarching mission, is that we
be united in love to the Trinity and to all other people. As we
live out the actions and words of godly love, that love
becomes more and more whole—perfected—in our lives.
Ultimately, we will live in this world in the very nature and
action of God. "As he is, so we are in this world." Can we
comprehend the magnificence of this? Are we willing to have
God's love living in the world through us?

1 John 4:11–18
Psalm 72:1–2,10,12–13
Mark 6:45–52

JANUARY 9

If anyone says, "I love God,"
but hates his brother, he is a liar;
for whoever does not love a brother whom he has seen
cannot love God whom he has not seen.
—1 JOHN 4:20

The writer of this letter is saying that real love happens in
the gritty daily details, not in the abstract regions of our
philosophy or good intentions. Dare I say that my love for
God is as strong as my love for the person I love the least.
Or, the disgust and judgment I feel for the person lowest on
my list is really an indication of how I feel about God. Wow.
Sometimes honesty hurts.

1 John 4:19—5:4
Psalm 72:1–2,14 and 15bc,17
Luke 4:14–22

JANUARY 10

*It happened that there was a man full of leprosy
in one of the towns where Jesus was;
and when he saw Jesus,
he fell prostrate, pleaded with him, and said,
"Lord, if you wish, you can make me clean."
Jesus stretched out his hand, touched him, and said,
"I do will it. Be made clean."
And the leprosy left him immediately.*
—LUKE 5:12–13

An "untouchable" approached Jesus and asked the impossible. "Full of leprosy" suggests a picture of absolute desolation, of decayed flesh, of stink and exhaustion. Jesus touched the man and healed him. We can ponder what it took for this man to approach the teacher. Sometimes the hardest thing we do is ask for help. It's a great risk, but God waits for us to come and ask.

1 John 5:5–13
Psalm 147:12–13,14–15,19–20
Luke 5:12–16

JANUARY 11

*We also know that the Son of God has come
and has given us discernment to know the one who is true.
And we are in the one who is true,
in his Son Jesus Christ.
He is the true God and eternal life.
Children, be on your guard against idols.*
—1 JOHN 5:20–21

We have been given discernment, but do we pay much attention to the inner workings of the Spirit? We are "in" Jesus, yet we are so tempted to seek the newest book or follow the speaker or teacher who is popular at the moment. Books and teachers are fine, but are we learning to listen to the One who is already within us? No surprise that the writer of this letter finishes with a warning against idolatry.

1 John 5:14–21
Psalm 149:1–2,3–4,5 and 6a and 9b
John 3:22–30

JANUARY 12

• THE BAPTISM OF THE LORD •

When the kindness and generous love
of God our savior appeared,
not because of any righteous deeds we had done
but because of his mercy,
he saved us through the bath of rebirth
and renewal by the Holy Spirit,
whom he richly poured out on us
through Jesus Christ our savior,
so that we might be justified by his grace
and become heirs in hope of eternal life.

—TITUS 3:4–7

Here is a beautiful summary of our salvation. I challenge you
to read this several times prayerfully, allowing these glorious
truths to move through your mind and heart.

Isaiah 40:1–5,9–11
Psalm 104:1b–2,3–4,24–25,27–28,29–30 (1)
Titus 2:11–14; 3:4–7
Luke 3:15–16,21–22

As he passed by the Sea of Galilee,
he saw Simon and his brother Andrew casting their nets into the sea:
they were fishermen.
Jesus said to them,
"Come after me, and I will make you fishers of men."
—MARK 1:16–17

I love that Jesus called people in the midst of their work. He didn't go looking for young men and women who were lingering in the marketplace, holding forth on their visions for the future. He looked for people who were already engaged in life, working hard, doing what they knew how to do. God looks for people who are already moving, knowing that a person in motion can be guided in one direction or another.

Hebrews 1:1–6
Psalm 97:1 and 2b,6 and 7c,9
Mark 1:14–20

JANUARY 14

He who consecrates
and those who are being consecrated all have one origin.
Therefore, he is not ashamed to call them "brothers," saying:
"I will proclaim your name to my brethren,
in the midst of the assembly I will praise you."
—HEBREWS 2:11–12

Do we fully comprehend what is being said here? Jesus, who consecrates us, and we who are consecrated, come from the same place. That is, we originated in the love and creativity of God. Jesus calls us brothers and sisters. May we enjoy more fully our identity as God's beloved children.

Hebrews 2:5–12
Psalm 8:2ab and 5,6–7,8–9
Mark 1:21–28

JANUARY 15

*Surely he did not help angels
but rather the descendants of Abraham;
therefore, he had to become like his brothers and sisters in every way,
that he might be a merciful and faithful high priest before God
to expiate the sins of the people.*
—HEBREWS 2:16–17

Lord Jesus, we cannot truly understand the miracle of your
becoming human like us, but we are grateful that you desired
to know us this intimately. When life becomes stressful and
painful, remind us that you do understand what we face.
Amen.

Hebrews 2:14–18
Psalm 105:1–2,3–4,6–7,8–9
Mark 1:29–39

*Encourage yourselves daily while it is still "today,"
so that none of you may grow hardened by the deceit of sin.*
—HEBREWS 3:13

What does it mean to grow hardened by the deceit of sin?
Is that hardness of heart an unwillingness to listen to
constructive criticism? Is it a weariness in doing what is good
and right? Is it impatience with the flaws and struggles of
others? Is it resistance to facing our own wrongdoings? The
antidote is to encourage one another. "Keep going—it's
worth it!" "Let's recall what Jesus said about this." "Have the
courage to look at yourself, trusting in God's mercy."
"Remember, you don't have to do this alone: My Father is
with you, and so am I."

Hebrews 3:7–14
Psalm 95:6–7c,8–9,10–11
Mark 1:40–45

Friday

JANUARY 17

• ST. ANTHONY, ABBOT •

What we have heard and know,
and what our fathers have declared to us,
we will declare to the generation to come
the glorious deeds of the LORD and his strength.

—PSALM 78:3–4

Young people learn from example, and when we focus on all the ways God has been with us, when we go about our days with evident faith in God's love, and when we focus on our hope in Christ—all of that makes an impact on children, teenagers, and young adults. They may not follow after us in churchgoing, but they certainly will know that it's possible to go through life with a spirit of gratitude and hope rather than bitterness and despair.

Hebrews 4:1–5,11
Psalm 78:3 and 4bc,6c–7,8
Mark 2:1–12

———————————

⇒ 48 ⇐

JANUARY 18

[Jesus] said to them,
"Those who are well do not need a physician, but the sick do."
—MARK 2:17

I confess that I have been guilty of expecting God to pay a lot of attention to my life, including what makes me sad, uncomfortable, tired, and so on. I have been a Christian for many years, and you'd think that by now I would remember that God loves me—a woman with a home, family, friends, and whose basic needs are satisfied—but God's primary focus remains on those yet to know the transformative power of forgiveness and love. The next time I fret over something not going my way, I ask that the Holy Spirit give me a little shake.

Hebrews 4:12–16
Psalm 19:8,9,10,15
Mark 2:13–17

Sunday

JANUARY 19

• SECOND SUNDAY IN ORDINARY TIME •

There was a wedding at Cana in Galilee,
and the mother of Jesus was there.
Jesus and his disciples were also invited to the wedding.
—JOHN 2:1–2

Well, we know what's coming, don't we? Jesus will turn water into wine and save the day at the wedding reception. But what was he doing at a wedding anyway? He was taking part in community, as any normal person would. At this point, Jesus knew there was a mission in front of him, on the cusp of beginning. But he went to the wedding that day simply to celebrate with others. Let's not forget to be "normal." Let's not underestimate the power of our ordinary community and connections. We never know what might be about to happen.

Isaiah 62:1–5
Psalm 96:1–2,2–3,7–8,9–10 (3)
1 Corinthians 12:4–11
John 2:1–11

JANUARY 20

[Jesus said,] "No one pours new wine into old wineskins.
Otherwise, the wine will burst the skins,
and both the wine and the skins are ruined.
Rather, new wine is poured into fresh wineskins."

—MARK 2:22

As we grow spiritually, understanding more and more of
God's ways, learning to see and think differently, being
transformed gradually into a more perfect image of God, our
old "containers" just won't work anymore. We must let go of
values and goals that are too small to accommodate grace.
We have to put away inadequate images of God and adopt
viewpoints and attitudes that expand as we gain wisdom.
Spiritual growth will not fit into our old manner of living. But
the old ways can be familiar and comfortable.
What will we choose?

Hebrews 5:1–10
Psalm 110:1,2,3,4
Mark 2:18–22

Tuesday

JANUARY 21

• ST. AGNES, VIRGIN AND MARTYR •

[Jesus] said to them,
"The sabbath was made for man, not man for the sabbath."
—MARK 2:27

It's good to occasionally reassess the way we do things, even our religious activities. If the way we do "church" is not helping us grow spiritually and participate fruitfully in the family of God, then it's time to figure out, prayerfully, what isn't working and why. The same goes for our personal rules about how we pray, do works of mercy, or contribute to our local parish. Our plans and systems must serve their ultimate purposes, rather than claim our unreflective allegiance.

Hebrews 6:10–20
Psalm 111:1–2,4–5,9 and 10c
Mark 2:23–28

JANUARY 22

• DAY OF PRAYER FOR THE LEGAL PROTECTION OF UNBORN CHILDREN •

Looking around at them with anger
and grieved at their hardness of heart,
Jesus said to the man, "Stretch out your hand."
He stretched it out and his hand was restored.
The Pharisees went out and immediately took counsel
with the Herodians against him to put him to death.

—MARK 3:5–6

Jesus challenged a religious system that had become burdensome for people, with too many rules to keep track of and with a focus on purity rather than on compassion. When a person becomes murderously hateful because of an act of mercy, clearly he or she has ceased to be motivated by God's love. These religious leaders planned to *kill* Jesus. Where today do we see such hatred, and how can we respond?

Hebrews 7:1–3,15–17
Psalm 110:1,2,3,4
Mark 3:1–6
Or, for the Day of Prayer, any readings from
the Mass "For Giving Thanks to God for the Gift of Human Life" or
the Mass "For Peace and Justice"

Sacrifice or oblation you wished not,
but ears open to obedience you gave me.
—PSALM 40:7

It's not so difficult to come up with works that make us look good. We have many opportunities to impress others; maybe we're also trying to impress God. But God simply waits until we stop our scheming and busyness. God waits for us to listen. We could do many things, but there is usually a certain thing God has in mind, something more meaningful, more fruitful than what we're trying to do.

Hebrews 7:25—8:6
Psalm 40:7–8a,8b–9,10,17
Mark 3:7–12

I will put my laws in their minds
and I will write them upon their hearts.
I will be their God,
and they shall be my people.
—HEBREWS 8:10

I learned a lot simply by being my parents' child. Absorbing their attitudes, taking on their viewpoints, learning, almost instinctively, their moral code—all of that was imprinted on my young heart and mind. Our heavenly Father desires such intimacy with us, such a close bond that we will quite naturally live out our holy nature.

Hebrews 8:6–13
Psalm 85:8 and 10,11–12,13–14
Mark 3:13–19

For steadfast is [the LORD's] kindness toward us,
and the fidelity of the LORD endures forever.
—PSALM 117:2

The apostle Paul would learn, over time, just how kind and
faithful was God who had knocked him down, blinded him,
and ushered him into a whole new life. Paul had to
recalibrate his beloved Jewish faith to include the Messiah,.
Jesus. He had to deal with persecution and hardship, with
fights among the faithful, and challenges to his authority to
preach the gospel. The stronger Paul became, the more
forcefully he spoke and wrote of God's love and faithfulness.
May we thank God for Paul today—and we can thank
St. Paul for allowing his life to demonstrate God's amazing
love for us.

Acts 22:3–16 or 9:1–22
Psalm 117:1bc,2
Mark 16:15–18

JANUARY 26

• THIRD SUNDAY IN ORDINARY TIME •

Ezra read plainly from the book of the law of God,
interpreting it so that all could understand what was read. . . .
"Today is holy to the LORD your God.
Do not be sad, and do not weep."
—NEHEMIAH 8:8–9

Are you ever discouraged when you read or hear Scripture?
Maybe you think, *There's no way I can live up to this* or *Where do*
I even begin? But God's word is given for our benefit. We can
be encouraged to learn how to live better, think more clearly,
and listen more attentively to what God speaks in Scripture
as well as in our hearts. Do not be sad or frightened to hear
from the God who loves you.

Nehemiah 8:2–4a,5–6,8–10
Psalm 19:8,9,10,15
1 Corinthians 12:12–30 or 12:12–14,27
Luke 1:1–4; 4:14–21

For Christ did not enter into a sanctuary made by hands,
a copy of the true one, but heaven itself,
that he might now appear before God on our behalf.
—HEBREWS 9:24

In the early days of God's people, there was a tabernacle where the priest could enter and offer sacrifice on behalf of the people. Then, centuries later, a grand temple where the priest would go into the holy of holies. But with the salvific work of Jesus the Christ, all temples have broken and flown apart to reveal the ultimate temple. Here it's called heaven, but we can call it the very realm and presence of God. With Christ there is no need for any holy place or altar; all has been made holy, and Christ remains in the Father's presence, constantly interceding for us.

Hebrews 9:15,24–28
Psalm 98:1,2–3ab,3cd–4,5–6
Mark 3:22–30

JANUARY 28

"Sacrifice and offering you did not desire,
but a body you prepared for me;
in burnt offerings and sin offerings you took no delight.
Then I said, As is written of me in the scroll,
Behold, I come to do your will, O God."
—HEBREWS 10:5–7

Blood sacrifices were discontinued in Judaism long ago, and
Christians never had such a practice. The temptation
remains, though, to try to do something to make up for our
sins and shortcomings. Whether it's severe penances of past
centuries or obsessive "spiritual" activities today, we feel
obligated to do what only Christ can do for us: restore our
relationship to God. Jesus, remind us of what you have
already accomplished.

Hebrews 10:1–10
Psalm 40:2 and 4ab,7–8a,10,11
Mark 3:31–35

Wednesday

JANUARY 29

"They are the people who hear the word,
but worldly anxiety, the lure of riches,
and the craving for other things intrude and choke the word,
and it bears no fruit."
—MARK 4:18–19

Holy Spirit, please help me notice when anxiety and "stuff"
and various cravings choke out the energy and desire I have
for an authentic and abiding friendship with you. Amen.

Hebrews 10:11–18
Psalm 110:1,2,3,4
Mark 4:1–20

JANUARY 30

Let us hold unwaveringly to our confession that gives us hope,
for he who made the promise is trustworthy.
We must consider how to rouse one another to love and good works.
—HEBREWS 10:23–24

Does your faith ever waver? Do you grow discouraged? Have
you lost sight of the faithful life you first desired? If so, then
you are normal. Why else would the writer of Hebrews
encourage the believers to hold on to their belief? Why the
exhortation to "rouse" one another to love and good works?
We are not meant to do this alone. And every saint and great
spiritual teacher has acknowledged the chronic temptation to
waver, to forget, to resist admitting that we need help from
our sisters and brothers.

Hebrews 10:19–25
Psalm 24:1–2,3–4ab,5–6
Mark 4:21–25

⇒ 61 ⇐

Friday

JANUARY 31

• ST. JOHN BOSCO, PRIEST •

[Jesus said to the crowds,]
"This is how it is with the Kingdom of God;
it is as if a man were to scatter seed on the land
and would sleep and rise night and day
and the seed would sprout and grow,
he knows not how."
—MARK 4:26–27

You and I have work to do. So we do it as faithfully as we know how. Then all we can do is watch and wait. We don't know how God is changing hearts and minds and lives, but all of that happens. The wonder is that we get to be a part of it. Thanks be to God!

Hebrews 10:32–39
Psalm 37:3–4,5–6,23–24,39–40
Mark 4:26–34

Saturday

FEBRUARY 1

All these died in faith.
They did not receive what had been promised
but saw it and greeted it from afar
and acknowledged themselves to be strangers and aliens on earth,
for those who speak thus show that they are seeking a homeland.
—HEBREWS 11:13–14

Have you planted any trees lately? If you're in your senior years, as I am, then you know that you won't live to see this tree in its greatest glory. You plant the tree because you see beyond your own life, your own generation. Our ancestors in the faith saw ahead to *us*, and their faithfulness to God made a way for us. This is the path all of us are walking to our ultimate homeland.

Hebrews 11:1–2,8–19
Luke 1:69–70,71–72,73–75
Mark 4:35–41

FEBRUARY 2

• THE PRESENTATION OF THE LORD •

When they had fulfilled all the prescriptions
of the law of the Lord,
they returned to Galilee, to their own town of Nazareth.
The child grew and became strong, filled with wisdom;
and the favor of God was upon him.
—LUKE 2:39–40

Presenting the infant Jesus to God in the temple was a high point for his Jewish parents. But then the real work began: they returned home and moved through daily life, year after year, growing, learning, bringing up their son and teaching him. His years of growth and formation were crucial—just as ours are.

Malachi 3:1–4
Psalm 24:7,8,9,10
Hebrews 2:14–18
Luke 2:22–40 or 2:22–32

Then the man went off and began to proclaim in the Decapolis what Jesus had done for him; and all were amazed.
—MARK 5:20

Jesus cast a "legion" of demons out of the man, so of course the man then wanted to go with Jesus. But Jesus told him to go back home to his family and tell them what the Lord had done for him. I can certainly understand the man wanting to leave; people in that area knew him as a crazy, dangerous, frightening person. How to begin rebuilding a life? Yet, this man now had credentials. His own experience with Jesus—his authentic story—gave him authority to speak, no matter his past. May we honor our own stories of what God has done for us.

Hebrews 11:32–40
Psalm 31:20,21,22,23,24
Mark 5:1–20

FEBRUARY 4

*Let the coming generation be told of the LORD
that they may proclaim to a people yet to be born
the justice he has shown.*
—PSALM 22:32

Certain stories regularly circulate through my family, and
they are stories of God's work in our lives. A
great-grandmother experienced healing; someone's life was
spared in a car crash; the prayers of others brought peace
during a time fraught with grief. Some of these stories go
back generations. They are part of our history as God's
people, and I am committed to keeping these stories going
for the generations to come.

Hebrews 12:1–4
Psalm 22:26b–27,28 and 30,31–32
Mark 5:21–43

Wednesday

FEBRUARY 5

• ST. AGATHA, VIRGIN AND MARTYR •

So strengthen your drooping hands and your weak knees.
Make straight paths for your feet,
that what is lame may not be dislocated but healed.
—HEBREWS 12:12–13

We bear some responsibility for our own spiritual health.
The writer of Hebrews points out that God can use our trials
to discipline and train us. It's normal to go through times of
weakness and disorientation, but how we respond matters.
Am I lame and stumbling? Perhaps it's time to make my path
straighter. God invites us to cooperate with divine love in
helping our lives grow strong and fruitful.

Hebrews 12:4–7,11–15
Psalm 103:1–2,13–14,17–18a
Mark 6:1–6

Thursday

FEBRUARY 6

• ST. PAUL MIKI AND COMPANIONS, MARTYRS •

Indeed, so fearful was the spectacle that Moses said,
"I am terrified and trembling."
—HEBREWS 12:21

Beware of the tame, domestic god—the one who always
makes you comfortable, who never demands too much, and
who doesn't ever leave you in the dark. Such a god is small
and false. Almighty God our Creator is not tamed by our
whims and expectations. Our God will lead us where we face
uncertainty and must trust in holy love to guide us.
Sometimes, we pay a very high price to be associated with
God, as did St. Paul Miki and so many other martyrs across
time. Will we be afraid at times? Yes. We might even be
terrified. Yet God is eternal and holds us
lovingly in that eternity.

Hebrews 12:18–19,21–24
Psalm 48:2–3ab,3cd–4,9,10–11
Mark 6:7–13

FEBRUARY 7

Your presence, O LORD, I seek.
Hide not your face from me;
do not in anger repel your servant.
You are my helper: cast me not off.
—PSALM 27:8–9

This is the prayer of one who understands that God responds
to us with love, even when there's good reason for anger.
Otherwise, this "servant" would not dare ask for God's
presence but would run away in fear. When I've truly made a
mess of things, I still long to see God's face because I know
that no other face, no other presence, will do. And, frankly, I
believe that God wants to see *my* face when I least feel
worthy of being seen.

Hebrews 13:1–8
Psalm 27:1,3,5,8b–9abc
Mark 6:14–29

Saturday

FEBRUARY 8

• ST. JEROME EMILIANI, PRIEST * ST. JOSEPHINE BAKHITA, VIRGIN •

*When Jesus disembarked and saw the vast crowd,
his heart was moved with pity for them,
for they were like sheep without a shepherd;
and he began to teach them many things.*

—MARK 6:34

Well, my response to a crowd is rarely pity! Crowds seem to reveal some of the worst qualities in people, and I am far more likely to have a judgmental attitude. Lord Jesus, please form in my heart the strong, steady love that will see our need for you. Amen.

Hebrews 13:15–17,20–21
Psalm 23:1–3a,3b–4,5,6
Mark 6:30–34

FEBRUARY 9

• FIFTH SUNDAY IN ORDINARY TIME •

When Simon Peter saw this, he fell at the knees of Jesus and said,
"Depart from me, Lord, for I am a sinful man."
—LUKE 5:8

Peter makes this statement right after the great catch of fish.
Peter can see that Jesus is no ordinary man. Furthermore, he
recognizes himself as "a sinful man." Jesus did not say
anything about sin, did he? This is a great example of how,
when we recognize God's presence, we recognize
immediately our own insufficiency, our flaws, our sins. This is
why evangelism is all about helping reveal God to others. It's
not our job to point out people's sins but to be a means of
their seeing God as a loving presence. Jesus drew Peter to
powerful love, which is what we can do for the people in
our lives.

Isaiah 6:1–2a,3–8
Psalm 138:1–2,2–3,4–5,7–8 (1c)
1 Corinthians 15:1–11 or 15:3–8,11
Luke 5:1–11

Monday

FEBRUARY 10

• ST. SCHOLASTICA, VIRGIN •

In the beginning, when God created the heavens and the earth,
the earth was a formless wasteland, and darkness covered the abyss,
while a mighty wind swept over the waters.
—GENESIS 1:1–2

Before creation, formlessness and darkness. We can carry this
image with us when we are going through painful change.
We don't know what will happen, and we can't come up with
a plan. Rather than enlightenment there is darkness in mind
and spirit. We are in a sorry state. But, wait. Just as a mighty
wind swept over the waters prior to the world's creation,
God's Spirit sweeps over the chaos and questions in our lives.
Something wonderful is about to happen. We can sit
expectantly in this formless darkness, knowing that the
mighty hand of God will do the work that is necessary for
that something to be accomplished.

Genesis 1:1–19
Psalm 104:1–2a,5–6,10 and 12,24 and 35c
Mark 6:53–56

FEBRUARY 11

• OUR LADY OF LOURDES •

*[Jesus said,] "You nullify the word of God
in favor of your tradition that you have handed on."*
—MARK 7:13

We must remember that Jesus was a practicing Jew. He went
to synagogue; from boyhood he had memorized large
portions of the Scriptures; he knew the law of Moses very
well. So, his argument was not with Judaism but with what
had been done to it. The Law had been wrapped in layers of
tradition to the point that what the Law really meant was lost
in favor of the tradition. We Christians are pretty good at
this too. We love our traditions, and we tend to impose
culture upon Scripture rather than allow Scripture to make us
a transforming force within the culture. May we ask on a
regular basis, What does God really desire?

Genesis 1:20—2:4a
Psalm 8:4–5,6–7,8–9
Mark 7:1–13

Jesus summoned the crowd again and said to them,
"Hear me, all of you, and understand.
Nothing that enters one from outside can defile that person;
but the things that come out from within are what defile."
—MARK 7:14–15

Notice that Jesus made an effort to gather the crowd around him, and he urged them to hear what he was saying. This was important. Also, let's remember that much of what Jesus had to contend with was a severe purity culture that did not represent all of Judaism but was a strong movement within it.

People were overly concerned about becoming contaminated—by unclean food, unclean people, non-Jews, and so on. I can't help but think about how, as a Christian, I have often avoided certain people with bad habits, who used strong language, and were simply different. This is a barrier Jesus wants knocked down.

Genesis 2:4b–9,15–17
Psalm 104:1–2a,27–28,29bc–30
Mark 7:14–23

FEBRUARY 13

Jesus went to the district of Tyre.
He entered a house and wanted no one to know about it,
but he could not escape notice.
—MARK 7:24

Sometimes Jesus wanted to maintain a low profile, but his efforts failed. When God's Spirit is at work through us, we cannot control its influence. Even Jesus had to adjust at times, so why shouldn't we?

Genesis 2:18–25
Psalm 128:1–2,3,4–5
Mark 7:24–30

When they heard the sound of the LORD God
moving about in the garden
at the breezy time of the day,
the man and his wife hid themselves from the LORD God
among the trees of the garden.

—GENESIS 3:8

Here's a simple principle for spiritual health. When you find
yourself avoiding God, stop! Why are you hiding? What are
you afraid of? Where can you possibly go to escape God?
What has made you angry or anxious? If necessary, talk to a
trusted friend or mentor about this. The sooner you stop
hiding and face what's going on, the less trouble you'll make
for yourself. And the sooner you can experience God's
compassion toward you.

Genesis 3:1–8
Psalm 32:1–2,5,6,7
Mark 7:31–37

FEBRUARY 15

When he expelled the man,
he settled him east of the garden of Eden;
and he stationed the cherubim and the fiery revolving sword,
to guard the way to the tree of life.
—GENESIS 3:24

When we don't take this story literally but as a sacred myth
given for our good, we discover good news in it. God has
moved Adam and Eve away from power they cannot yet
understand nor use wisely. There are universes of knowledge
and understanding that are not yet available to us. Jesus the
Christ has brought us closer to the mystery, and the Holy
Spirit continues to teach us. In the meantime, we are invited
to trust God's tender keeping of us. The two humans were
outside the garden, but God had created everything outside
the garden too.

Genesis 3:9–24
Psalm 90:2,3–4abc,5–6,12–13
Mark 8:1–10

Sunday

FEBRUARY 16

• SIXTH SUNDAY IN ORDINARY TIME •

Blessed is the one who trusts in the LORD,
whose hope is in the LORD.
He is like a tree planted beside the waters
that stretches out its roots to the stream.
—JEREMIAH 17:7–8

God does not want our trust because God's divine ego needs it. God wants us to find our true source, like a tree whose roots seek out water. God does not need our need for God! God desires that we grow and flourish, and that's why God invites us again and again to turn our roots to the source. May we notice when we are seeking elsewhere.

Jeremiah 17:5–8
Psalm 1:1–2,3,4 and 6 (40:5a)
1 Corinthians 15:12,16–20
Luke 6:17,20–26

⇒ 78 ⇐

The LORD then said: "What have you done!
Listen: your brother's blood cries out to me from the soil!"
—GENESIS 4:10

A lot of people in this world die horrible deaths—from
abuse, starvation, genocide, murder. We do well to grieve
those deaths and to do what justice we can. We do even
better to trust that God hears the cry of spilled blood. No
evil escapes God's notice, and no life ends without God's
knowledge and mercy. As we work for justice as well as we
are able, may we thank God for mercy that sees beyond our
own sight.

Genesis 4:1–15,25
Psalm 50:1 and 8,16bc–17,20–21
Mark 8:11–13

FEBRUARY 18

The voice of the LORD is over the waters,
the LORD, over vast waters.
—PSALM 29:3

When we stand upon a wild seashore and feel how small
and powerless we are, we can remind ourselves that the great
energy or fierceness of creation is God's voice,
God's presence.

Genesis 6:5–8; 7:1–5,10
Psalm 29:1a and 2,3ac–4,3b and 9c–10
Mark 8:14–21

Then [Jesus] laid hands on the man's eyes a second time
and he saw clearly;
his sight was restored and he could see everything distinctly.
—MARK 8:25

So, Jesus laid his hands on this man twice before the man's
vision was restored completely. Why is this story in the
Gospels? You'd think that those who compiled stories of
Jesus would have skipped this one because it seems that Jesus'
healing power did not work entirely the first time around. Is
the message here that sometimes healing is complex and
happens in stages? That would certainly ring true in the lives
of people I've known. The point is not that Jesus twice laid
on hands but that, ultimately, the man could see.

Genesis 8:6–13,20–22
Psalm 116:12–13,14–15,18–19
Mark 8:22–26

FEBRUARY 20

Then Peter took [Jesus] aside and began to rebuke him.
At this he turned around and, looking at his disciples,
rebuked Peter and said, "Get behind me, Satan.
You are thinking not as God does, but as human beings do."
—MARK 8:32–33

Jesus sometimes shocked people simply by telling the larger truth they had failed to see. He knew that the human viewpoint was limited and therefore inaccurate and capable of doing much damage. Otherwise, he would not have been so sharp with Peter in this instance. The disciples needed—and we, today, need—to open hearts to the ever-expanding truth of God's great love for us. Such love can withstand trial and tribulation, and so that love must at times correct our impulse to escape hard times.

Genesis 9:1–13
Psalm 102:16–18,19–21,22–23, and 29.
Mark 8:27–33

Friday

FEBRUARY 21

• ST. PETER DAMIAN, BISHOP AND DOCTOR OF THE CHURCH •

Thus the LORD scattered them from there all over the earth,
and they stopped building the city.
—GENESIS 11:8

I find myself saying these days, "So, did God not see the
Internet coming? Did God not see AI (artificial intelligence)
coming?" I weary of people's panic and fear over
technological progress. But we should not forget today's
lesson, the story of the tower of Babel, the people's great
effort to create a place from which their combined power
and knowledge would grow immensely. God confused their
language and scattered them. To what end is our progress
taking us? What is our responsibility in how we use it?

Genesis 11:1–9
Psalm 33:10–11,12–13,14–15
Mark 8:34—9:1

≥ 83 ≤

You spread the table before me
in the sight of my foes.
—PSALM 23:5

Let's pause and consider the picture the psalmist gives us
here. With enemies all around, God spreads out a feast and
serves me a meal. You'd think that God would take me
completely out of enemy territory before feeding me, but no.
God's mercy and power are so reliable that I can enjoy my
life even when everything around me feels hostile and
dangerous. Am I willing to receive God's goodness while in a
place of sorrow, fear, or danger? Could it be that God is
teaching me holy courage?

1 Peter 5:1–4
Psalm 23:1–3a,4,5,6
Matthew 16:13–19

FEBRUARY 23

• SEVENTH SUNDAY IN ORDINARY TIME •

[Jesus said,] "Stop judging and you will not be judged.
Stop condemning and you will not be condemned.
Forgive and you will be forgiven."

—LUKE 6:37

We can read these words of Jesus as a simple equation: what I do to others will be done to me. But I think there is a deeper dynamic here. My lack of condemnation, and my willingness to forgive, create an environment in which better qualities can flourish. My acceptance of others frees them to stop worrying about what I think and simply be themselves. They can lower their defenses when they're with me rather than become defensive and respond with their own judgment and condemnation. Jesus understood how powerful one person's presence, attitude, and actions can be. We can pray to become a freeing presence to others.

1 Samuel 26:2,7–9,12–13,22–23
Psalm 103:1–2,3–4,8,10,12–13 (8a)
1 Corinthians 15:45–49
Luke 6:27–38

When [Jesus] entered the house, his disciples asked him in private,
"Why could we not drive the spirit out?"
He said to them, "This kind can only come out through prayer."
—MARK 9:28–29

When it appears that we have become spiritually ineffective, it's good to ask Jesus why. Perhaps what we pray for is not the best outcome after all. Perhaps we need to draw closer to God, in prayer, to receive the resources necessary. And, sometimes, we have taken on a responsibility that's not really ours. "Why?" is not an impertinent question to send God's way. Divine love welcomes our questions and our seeking.

Sirach 1:1–10
Psalm 93:1ab,1cd–2,5
Mark 9:14–29

Tuesday

FEBRUARY 25

My son, when you come to serve the LORD,
stand in justice and fear,
prepare yourself for trials.
—SIRACH 2:1

Where did we ever get the idea that life with God would be problem free? We carry that idea deep within us, and here's how I know: when trouble comes, we always wonder whose fault it is. We assume that there's something wrong because we're not happy. This is shallow spirituality. A bit further down (Sirach 2:4), this passage in Sirach tells us to "accept whatever befalls you, when sorrowful, be steadfast, and in crushing misfortune be patient." God means to shape us through trials, as precious metals are refined by fire.

Therefore, let's not panic on the bad days.

Sirach 2:1–11
Psalm 37:3–4,18–19,27–28,39–40
Mark 9:30–37

John said to Jesus,
"Teacher, we saw someone driving out demons in your name,
and we tried to prevent him because he does not follow us."
—MARK 9:38

Through the ages, the Holy Spirit has demonstrated that
God will work with anyone anywhere, that God responds to
the heart that seeks relationship. Jesus did mighty works
wherever he found faith. Yet many Christians become
obsessed with how other Christians practice their faith. We
are beset by an us/them attitude. I encourage you to read
Jesus' response to John in this Mark 9 passage.

Sirach 4:11–19
Psalm 119:165,168,171,172,174,175
Mark 9:38–40

FEBRUARY 27

• ST. GREGORY OF NAREK, ABBOT AND DOCTOR OF THE CHURCH •

[Jesus said to his disciples,]
"Whoever causes one of these little ones who believe in me to sin,
it would be better for him if a great millstone
were put around his neck
and he were thrown into the sea."
—MARK 9:42

Jesus may have been referring to children, but it's also likely that "little ones" here means anyone who, like a child, is powerless, marginalized, humble. The point is, don't get in the way of another person's faith. Don't do anything to discourage a person from accepting God's love and following the way of Jesus. How do we discourage others spiritually? By discounting their stories, by heaping lots of rules on them, by belittling their still young and forming faith. We love others by encouraging and affirming whatever spiritual growth they are experiencing.

Sirach 5:1–8
Psalm 1:1–2,3,4 and 6
Mark 9:41–50

A kind mouth multiplies friends and appeases enemies,
and gracious lips prompt friendly greetings.
—SIRACH 6:5

A couple of years ago, my husband and I relocated from
Chicago to Springdale, Arkansas. I've always been proud of
how friendly Chicagoans are, but folks in the Ozarks have
turned kind speech into an art form. It is so easy to converse
with total strangers here. Friendliness and welcome form the
starting point for people's words and facial expressions. It
really does make a difference. How often do I forget the
power of a simple positive greeting and a smile?

Sirach 6:5–17
Psalm 119:12,16,18,27,34,35
Mark 10:1–12

MARCH 1

*People were bringing children to Jesus that he might touch them,
but the disciples rebuked them.*
—MARK 10:13

No doubt the disciples thought that Jesus had more
important work to do than blessing children. After all, he
healed people and cast out demons. These children and their
mothers were a distraction. And, frankly, men of the time
considered women and children extensions of themselves,
more or less property. Jesus must help his disciples unlearn
long-held beliefs and attitudes. In a world where children
had no rights or power, Jesus asserted that they were
examples to the adults, that God highly favored these
little ones.

Sirach 17:1–15
Psalm 103:13–14,15–16,17–18
Mark 10:13–16

Sunday

MARCH 2

The fruit of a tree shows the care it has had;
so too does one's speech disclose the bent of one's mind.
—SIRACH 27:6

The mouth might tell a lie, but our speech will ultimately
reveal the truth about who we are. What do I really think?
What makes me angry or defensive? When am I most likely
to be impatient and short-tempered? All comes out through
my words and their tone. In fact, sometimes those who hear
me know I'm angry before I know it—or am willing to admit
it. Which means that I need to pay attention to what others
hear me say and how my words affect them. Just another
aspect of self-awareness.

Sirach 27:4–7
Psalm 92:2–3,13–14,15–16
1 Corinthians 15:54–58
Luke 6:39–45

Monday

MARCH 3

Jesus, looking at him, loved him and said to him,
"You are lacking in one thing.
Go, sell what you have, and give to the poor
and you will have treasure in heaven; then come, follow me."
—MARK 10:21

Jesus looked at a wealthy man—a conscientious, faithful Jew—and saw the one thing that stood in his way to a full life with God. St. Ignatius of Loyola would say that Jesus saw the man's remaining area of unfreedom, the part of his life he still clung to. In this way he looks at each of us and sees what still holds on to us, what still saps our energy or distracts us from our faith. I like to think that, eventually, that rich man did sell all he had and followed Jesus. What keeps you from walking beside Jesus today?

Sirach 17:20–24
Psalm 32:1–2,5,6,7
Mark 10:17–27

Give to the Most High as he has given to you,
generously, according to your means.
—SIRACH 35:12

Recently, my husband and I helped some people over several
weeks, and it was a good lesson for me in what generosity is.
I usually worry over finances, but at this time I chose not to
worry but simply give what seemed right and trust that the
money would work out eventually. "According to your
means" is an important phrase. My means are quite different
from that of others, and what I see as a low bank account
balance is for some enough money to help them breathe
freely for a few days. Generosity is actually an increase of
faith, isn't it?

Sirach 35:1–12
Psalm 50:5–6,7–8,14 and 23
Mark 10:28–31

We implore you on behalf of Christ,
be reconciled to God.
For our sake he made him to be sin who did not know sin,
so that we might become the righteousness of God in him.
—2 CORINTHIANS 5:20B–21

God has made a fundamental change in the universe through the life, death, and resurrection of Jesus the Christ. But do we really think about this from day to day—that in some cosmological, mystical way, God exchanged sin for righteousness? God made it possible for us to be part of Christ, to belong to his body. We have access to *righteousness*—can we even comprehend it? The least we can do is remind ourselves of what Christ accomplished for us.

Joel 2:12–18
Psalm 51:3–4,5–6ab,12–13,14 and 17
2 Corinthians 5:20—6:2
Matthew 6:1–6,16–18

———————

Thursday

MARCH 6

• THURSDAY AFTER ASH WEDNESDAY •

[Jesus said to his disciples,]
"The Son of Man must suffer greatly and be rejected
by the elders, the chief priests, and the scribes,
and be killed and on the third day be raised."
—LUKE 9:22

Imagine that a teacher among us today made many priests,
bishops, and even the pope uncomfortable and angry with
him. To speak the truth and follow God's path for him,
Jesus—who loved the faith of his Jewish ancestors—had to
be willing to alienate all those religious leaders on whom the
people relied. This was a radical path, and we must never
forget it. Sometimes God asks us to do what is
highly unpopular.

Deuteronomy 30:15–20
Psalm 1:1–2,3,4 and 6
Luke 9:22–25

Friday

MARCH 7

• FRIDAY AFTER ASH WEDNESDAY
ST. PERPETUA AND ST. FELICITY, MARTYRS •

They seek me day after day,
and desire to know my ways,
Like a nation that has done what is just
and not abandoned the law of their God.
—ISAIAH 58:2

Did you know that even if you seek God and honestly want
to know God's ways, God might not respond to you? This
was the situation Isaiah addressed. The people ignored the
needs of others and neglected justice, but they still really
wanted God in their lives. The problem? They refused to do
what they *already knew* God wanted, which was to care for
others and to do justice.

Isaiah 58:1–9a
Psalm 51:3–4,5–6ab,18–19
Matthew 9:14–15

If you remove from your midst oppression,
false accusation and malicious speech;
If you bestow your bread on the hungry
and satisfy the afflicted;
Then light shall rise for you in the darkness,
and the gloom shall become for you like midday;
Then the LORD will guide you always
and give you plenty even on the parched land.
—ISAIAH 58:9B–11A

Do you want to know what God's will is? Isaiah was clear centuries ago, and the message has not changed. If not, what can you do to make yourself ready?

Isaiah 58:9b–14
Psalm 86:1–2,3–4,5–6
Luke 5:27–32

Sunday

MARCH 9

The devil said to him,
"If you are the Son of God,
command this stone to become bread."
Jesus answered him,
"It is written, One does not live on bread alone."
—LUKE 4:3–4

The temptations were real for Jesus—he was truly tempted to do what the devil suggested, otherwise these wouldn't have been tests at all. After an extended fast, Jesus was hungry, likely beginning to starve. Logically, there wasn't anything wrong with turning stones into bread. But he knew that anything that drew him away from the Father was a spiritual danger. Also, he knew who was making the suggestion: the one who wanted Jesus' mission to fail. It's wise to ask ourselves who is behind the solutions offered us.

Deuteronomy 26:4–10
Psalm 91:1–2,10–11,12–13,14–15
Romans 10:8–13
Luke 4:1–13

Monday

MARCH 10

Take no revenge and cherish no grudge against your fellow countrymen.
You shall love your neighbor as yourself.
—LEVITICUS 19:18

Revenge and grudges: we are immersed in these mentalities.
How many movies have vengeance as the main theme? How
many assaults and murders are the fruit of grudge-holding?
And how many political moves are simply means of getting
back at opponents? If we stand for God's way, we will
automatically become opposed to so much that people do
and say in this world. But if we won't stand up, who will?

Leviticus 19:1–2,11–18
Psalm 19:8,9,10,15
Matthew 25:31–46

Tuesday

MARCH 11

When the just cry out, the LORD hears them,
and from all their distress he rescues them.
The LORD is close to the brokenhearted,
and those who are crushed in spirit he saves.
—PSALM 34:18–19

We can take our cues from the Lord about what is important.
God moves us toward justice and compassion, always. In fact,
in most cases, we can discern the best thing to do by asking,
"What would be most just?" or "What would compassion look
like in this situation?"

Isaiah 55:10–11
Psalm 34:4–5,6–7,16–17,18–19
Matthew 6:7–15

Wednesday

MARCH 12

*When God saw by their actions how they turned from their evil way,
he repented of the evil that he had threatened to do to them;
he did not carry it out.*
—JONAH 3:10

The sacred stories show us a God who is not static and
nonresponsive. Throughout the Scriptures we see a God who
desires interaction with people, whether individuals or entire
nations. God will interact with you and me if we simply
listen and open our hearts.

Jonah 3:1–10
Psalm 51:3–4,12–13,18–19
Luke 11:29–32

*[Esther said,] "Help me, who am alone and have no help but you,
for I am taking my life in my hand."*
—ESTHER C:14–15

Esther was literally taking her life in her hand; her actions
might result in her execution. Yet she was convinced that her
course of action was right. She had no one to back her up,
there in the king's palace. She was just a wife, and a foreigner
at that. I love this story because it shows us a truly fearless
woman. I believe we are all called to be fearless as we do
God's work in the world. It doesn't mean that we don't feel
fear and anxiety but that our confidence in God enables us to
move forward in faith.

Esther C:12,14–16,23–25
Psalm 138:1–2ab,2cde–3,7c–8
Matthew 7:7–12

*"Therefore, if you bring your gift to the altar, . . .
go first and be reconciled with your brother,
and then come and offer your gift."*
—MATTHEW 5:23–24

Our communion with God cannot be separated from our
communion with other people. This is a difficult principle,
but we see it throughout God's word. Here, Jesus is being
quite direct about how much it matters to settle the
differences among ourselves. A break between me and
another person forms a break between me and God, who
loves that other person. God's love for me never wavers, but
my ability to receive that love can be disrupted by my
ongoing quarrel with a brother or sister.

Ezekiel 18:21–28
Psalm 130:1–2,3–4,5–7a,7bc–8
Matthew 5:20–26

MARCH 15

"But I say to you, love your enemies,
and pray for those who persecute you,
that you may be children of your heavenly Father,
for he makes his sun rise on the bad and the good,
and causes the rain to fall on the just and the unjust."
—MATTHEW 5:44–45

My sister told me about the time she asked God to get rid of people belonging to a certain terrorist group because of all the pain they were causing. But she felt God saying to her, "I love those people, too." Then she began to pray for them. Yes, our prayers are meant for those who need them most.

Deuteronomy 26:16–19
Psalm 119:1–2,4–5,7–8
Matthew 5:43–48

*He will change our lowly body
to conform with his glorified body
by the power that enables him also
to bring all things into subjection to himself.*
—PHILIPPIANS 3:21

Lord Jesus, may I always remember that your constant
movement is this: to bring all things into subjection to
yourself. In bringing me to yourself, you will transform even
this body into a glorified version of itself. Remind me that
my future continues in you, and it will be marvelous.

Genesis 15:5–12,17–18
Psalm 27:1,7–8,8–9,13–14 (1a)
Philippians 3:17—4:1 or 3:20—4:1
Luke 9:28b–36

MARCH 17

• ST. PATRICK, BISHOP •

Let the prisoners' sighing come before you;
with your great power free those doomed to death.
—PSALM 79:11

St. Patrick was a prisoner who, after getting free, returned to the country of his imprisonment to share the gospel of Jesus. Today, let's remember all who languish in prisons around the world, that the light of Christ might come to them.

Daniel 9:4b–10
Psalm 79:8,9,11 and 13
Luke 6:36–38

Tuesday

MARCH 18

• ST. CYRIL OF JERUSALEM, BISHOP AND DOCTOR OF THE CHURCH •

Jesus spoke to the crowds and to his disciples, saying,
"The scribes and the Pharisees
have taken their seat on the chair of Moses.
Therefore, do and observe all things whatsoever they tell you,
but do not follow their example."
—MATTHEW 23:1–3

We can honor our faith and follow Jesus—while refusing to
follow the example of leaders who do not honor God, the
church, or the faith. We can remain in the church even while
some in the church do wrong. Jesus encourages us in our
path toward faith but warns us against bad examples.

Isaiah 1:10,16–20
Psalm 50:8–9,16bc–17,21 and 23
Matthew 23:1–12

MARCH 19

• ST. JOSEPH, SPOUSE OF THE BLESSED VIRGIN MARY •

Each year Jesus' parents went to Jerusalem for the feast of Passover,
and when he was twelve years old,
they went up according to festival custom.
—LUKE 2:41–42

Joseph and Mary brought up Jesus in the Jewish faith and traditions; we cannot underestimate the influence of all those years of prayers, teachings, pilgrimages, and festivals. Jesus' journey began in the context of "ordinary" religious life, and we can thank Mary his mother and Joseph his foster father for this.

2 Samuel 7:4–5a,12–14a,16
Psalm 89:2–3,4–5,27 and 29
Romans 4:13,16–18,22
Matthew 1:16,18–21,24a or Luke 2:41–51a

Thursday

MARCH 20

When the poor man died,
he was carried away by angels to the bosom of Abraham.
—LUKE 16:22

Isn't it interesting that, in the story Jesus tells here, the poor man automatically goes to the bosom of Abraham. All we know of him is that, in his life on earth, he was desperately poor. It's almost as if Jesus is saying that God's priority is to comfort those who suffer and who are poor. What are we to make of this? Why did Jesus use this example when talking with the Pharisees?

Jeremiah 17:5–10
Psalm 1:1–2,3,4 and 6
Luke 16:19–31

*When the LORD called down a famine on the land
and ruined the crop that sustained them,
He sent a man before them,
Joseph, sold as a slave.*
—PSALM 105:16–17

We never know whom God will call out to do a mighty work or save an entire people. In this case, the young man whose brothers had sold him into slavery to get rid of him becomes a ruler in his own right, placed precisely so that he could, at a future time, save his father's people. The question is, Will we recognize such people when they arrive to help us?

Genesis 37:3–4,12–13a,17b–28a
Psalm 105:16–17,18–19,20–21
Matthew 21:33–43,45–46

*Tax collectors and sinners were all drawing near to listen to Jesus,
but the Pharisees and scribes began to complain, saying,
"This man welcomes sinners and eats with them."*
—LUKE 15:1–2

Am I ever in danger of being talked about because I hang out
with the "wrong" people? And, if not, is that a good thing?
Sometimes we Christians are too sensitive to what others
might think of us. We're also too afraid to be around people
who are different from us, especially if they are people of
questionable character. Seems we are doing the opposite of
what Jesus did. Worth thinking about.

Micah 7:14–15,18–20
Psalm 103:1–2,3–4,9–10,11–12
Luke 15:1–3,11–32

⇒ 112 ⇐

Sunday

MARCH 23

• THIRD SUNDAY OF LENT •

Jesus said to them in reply,
"Do you think that because these Galileans suffered in this way
they were greater sinners than all other Galileans?
By no means!
But I tell you, if you do not repent,
you will all perish as they did!"
—LUKE 13:2

We'd like to think that the really awful tragedies happen to
people who deserve them, yet we know this is not the case.
When it comes to sin, there's relatively little difference
between one person and another, in that any sin separates us
from God. I think Jesus is making the point that no one is
without sin and that our sinful ways create a world in which
horrible things happen. Our appropriate
response is repentance.

Exodus 3:1–8a,13–15
Psalm 103:1–2,3–4,6–7,8,11 (8a)
1 Corinthians 10:1–6,10–12
Luke 13:1–9

But Naaman went away angry, saying,
"I thought that he would surely come out and stand there
to invoke the LORD his god,
and would move his hand over the spot,
and thus cure the leprosy."
—2 KINGS 5:11

God's prophet instructed Naaman to wash in the Jordan
River to cleanse away his leprosy, but Naaman had other
ideas about how he should be healed. How often do we cling
to our own expectations of how God should help us?

2 Kings 5:1–15b
Psalm 42:2–3; 43:3–4
Luke 4:24–30

Tuesday

MARCH 25

• THE ANNUNCIATION OF THE LORD •

And the angel said to [Mary] in reply,
"The Holy Spirit will come upon you,
and the power of the Most High will overshadow you."
—LUKE 1:35

We stand in awe of Mary, who acquiesced to the Holy
Spirit's work in her life. But consider this: the Holy Spirit
wants to work in us, too, invites us to participate in what
God is doing all around us. You and I have the continuing
opportunity to say yes to God's work in us.

Isaiah 7:10–14; 8:10
Psalm 40:7–8a,8b–9,10,11
Hebrews 10:4–10
Luke 1:26–38

Wednesday

MARCH 26

*"Take care and be earnestly on your guard
not to forget the things which your own eyes have seen,
nor let them slip from your memory as long as you live."*
—DEUTERONOMY 4:9

Sometimes I wonder if the angels have nicknames for us
humans. If they did, I'm sure one of those names would be
"forgetful ones," because we allow so much valuable history
to slip out of memory. We forget how God has moved
among us, how the Holy Spirit has comforted and taught us,
how the truth has been revealed to us again and again.
Dear Holy Spirit, continue to remind us of what we have
seen with our own eyes.

Deuteronomy 4:1,5–9
Psalm 147:12–13,15–16,19–20
Matthew 5:17–19

⋚ 116 ⋜

Thursday

MARCH 27

Oh, that today you would hear his voice:
"Harden not your hearts as at Meribah,
as in the day of Massah in the desert,
where your fathers tempted me;
they tested me though they had seen my works."
—PSALM 95:7–9

Have you ever met someone with a hard heart? Someone
who refuses to learn new information or listen to wisdom or
make any kind of change, especially a change of mind? Once
we grow hard in our opinions and decisions, it can be
difficult to shift direction. The longer our hearts remain hard,
the more harsh and acute any kind of change will be. Lord,
help us change now, this moment, and not wait any longer.

Jeremiah 7:23–28
Psalm 95:1–2,6–7,8–9
Luke 11:14–23

"Thus says the LORD:
Return, O Israel, to the LORD, your God;
you have collapsed through your guilt."
—HOSEA 14:2

When I think of all the ways guilt affects people, "collapsed"
is one of many. Guilt causes us to hide, to lie, to avoid
people, to turn inward, to simmer in shame, to blame others,
to see the whole world in a cynical, hopeless way. No
wonder God calls for us to return. Sin and guilt have
damaged us, and only God can bring healing and restoration.

Hosea 14:2–10
Psalm 81:6c–8a,8bc–9,10–11ab,14 and 17
Mark 12:28–34

Saturday

MARCH 29

My sacrifice, O God, is a contrite spirit;
a heart contrite and humbled, O God, you will not spurn.
—PSALM 51:19

How much does it cost me to admit fault and say, "Sorry"? A
few moments' embarrassment? A turn toward humility? That's
not a great cost for freedom, healing, and a fresh start, is it?

Hosea 6:1–6
Psalm 51:3–4,18–19,20–21ab
Luke 18:9–14

Sunday

MARCH 30

• FOURTH SUNDAY OF LENT •

And all this is from God,
who has reconciled us to himself through Christ
and given us the ministry of reconciliation,
namely, God was reconciling the world to himself in Christ, . . .
So we are ambassadors for Christ,
as if God were appealing through us.
—2 CORINTHIANS 5:18–20

Christ our savior, make us bold to represent you to others, to
allow God to appeal to them through our words, actions,
expressions, and presence. We humbly ask to become
channels of your love.

Joshua 5:9a,10–12
Psalm 34:2–3,4–5,6–7 (9a)
2 Corinthians 5:17–21
Luke 15:1–3,11–32

They shall live in the houses they build,
and eat the fruit of the vineyards they plant.
—ISAIAH 65:21

The Lord is describing the new heaven and new earth:
people who can build houses and live in them, cultivate food
and harvest it. These seem to be simple pleasures, but the
ability to live safely and eat sufficiently is denied many
people in this world. Those of us who have a home and food
would do well to remember what a privilege it is—in fact, it's
a taste of paradise.

Isaiah 65:17–21
Psalm 30:2 and 4,5–6,11–12a and 13b
John 4:43–54

Tuesday

APRIL 1

One man was there who had been ill for thirty-eight years.
When Jesus saw him lying there
and knew that he had been ill for a long time, he said to him,
"Do you want to be well?"
—JOHN 5:5–6

The man in this story had been ill for thirty-eight years, but
in the next verse, he tells Jesus that there's no one to help
him into the water. I have to ask, "What kind of person
cannot find anyone else, in so many years, to help him?"
What kept others from approaching him? Was he bitter,
proud? Did he secretly enjoy being a victim? Little wonder
Jesus asked if he wanted to be well. Jesus knew that
sometimes, we don't really want to change. We resist truth,
healing, the help of others. What would be your response
today if Jesus asked you, "Do you want to be well?"

Ezekiel 47:1–9,12
Psalm 46:2–3,5–6,8–9
John 5:1–16

Wednesday

APRIL 2

• ST. FRANCIS OF PAOLA, HERMIT •

Can a mother forget her infant,
be without tenderness for the child of her womb?
Even should she forget,
I will never forget you.
—ISAIAH 49:15

The prophet uses the most tender language to describe God's love for the people. It matters a lot—the images we use for God. What images for God have encouraged you? What images of God have not been so positive for you?

Isaiah 49:8–15
Psalm 145:8–9,13cd–14,17–18
John 5:17–30

APRIL 3

*"You search the Scriptures,
because you think you have eternal life through them;
even they testify on my behalf.
But you do not want to come to me to have life."*
—JOHN 5:39–40

These are strong words from Jesus. Those who relied on the
sacred Scriptures but who rejected him did not attain the life
they sought. How many people today still use Scripture to
prove their opinions, to cast judgment on others, to decide
who is or is not a Christian, or to claim their own
righteousness? The real proof is our reliance on Jesus the
Christ and our willingness to follow him.

Exodus 32:7–14
Psalm 106:19–20,21–22,23
John 5:31–47

Friday

APRIL 4

• ST. ISIDORE OF SEVILLE, BISHOP AND DOCTOR OF THE CHURCH •

Jesus moved about within Galilee;
he did not wish to travel in Judea,
because the Jews were trying to kill him.
—JOHN 7:1

When Pope Francis was Jorge Bergoglio and archbishop of
Buenos Aires, one of the village priests received death threats
because he dared speak out against those responsible for
bringing illegal drugs into the community. He went to the
archbishop with his dilemma. Bergoglio paused, then said,
"First of all we must be calm because we are acting in
harmony with the gospel." As in Jesus' day, those who speak
the truth and stand up for what is right often anger those
who do wrong. May we pray this day for all who live under
threat for Jesus' sake.

Wisdom 2:1a,12–22
Psalm 34:17–18,19–20,21 and 23
John 7:1–2,10,25–30

Saturday

APRIL 5

• ST. VINCENT FERRER, PRIEST •

Do me justice, O LORD, because I am just,
and because of the innocence that is mine.
Let the malice of the wicked come to an end,
but sustain the just.
O searcher of heart and soul, O just God.
—PSALM 7:9B–10

Sometimes a person knows that she is in the right, has done no wrong, and yet others go after her, causing trouble and laying blame. And sometimes, all that person can do is cry out to God, who knows every heart and sees the entire truth of the matter. Lord God, remind us to entrust to you our circumstances and reputations.

Jeremiah 11:18–20
Psalm 7:2–3,9bc–10,11–12
John 7:40–53

Sunday

APRIL 6

• FIFTH SUNDAY OF LENT •

It is not that I have already taken hold of it
or have already attained perfect maturity,
but I continue my pursuit in hope that I may possess it,
since I have indeed been taken possession of by Christ Jesus.

—PHILIPPIANS 3:12

We are not meant to be passive observers of God's actions in
this world. We are meant to participate with God,
collaborate in this majestic, ongoing creation. This is a goal
worth hoping for and working toward.
This is a worthy ambition.

Isaiah 43:16–21
Psalm 126:1–2,2–3,4–5,6 (3)
Philippians 3:8–14
John 8:1–11
Or, for Year A, Ezekiel 37:12–14/Romans 8:8–11/John 11:1–45
or 11:3–7, 17, 20–27, 33b–45 (34)

Jesus answered, "You know neither me nor my Father.
If you knew me, you would know my Father also."
—JOHN 8:19

The character of divine love is consistent. People who
understood God the Father would recognize the same traits
in Jesus, and Jesus knew this. We can recognize divine love in
others rather than quibble about the details of their beliefs.
True beliefs show themselves in actions.

Daniel 13:1–9,15–17,19–30,33–62 or 13:41c–62
Psalm 23:1–3a,3b–4,5,6
John 8:12–20

Tuesday

APRIL 8

With their patience worn out by the journey,
the people complained against God and Moses,
"Why have you brought us up from Egypt to die in this desert,
where there is no food or water?
We are disgusted with this wretched food!"
—NUMBERS 21:4–5

Has your patience ever been worn out by the journey? Mine
sure has. Daily life can become such a slog, and sometimes a
person just wants everything to be different and new. The
journey of faith requires work, determination, patience, and
hope. Just for today, offer your steps to
the God who leads you.

Numbers 21:4–9
Psalm 102:2–3,16–18,19–21
John 8:21–30

Wednesday

APRIL 9

*"I see four men unfettered and unhurt,
walking in the fire, and the fourth looks like a son of God."*
—DANIEL 3:92

Three young Hebrew men were thrown into a fire because
they refused to worship a human king. As it turned out, God
spared them, but they still had to go into the fire. This serves
as an important reminder to me: I may have to walk into
situations assuming they will be painful. That is, at times I
will walk right toward suffering, simply because it's the right
thing to do. Maybe God will spare me, maybe not. But my
steps should be steadfast regardless.

Daniel 3:14–20,91–92,95
Daniel 3:52,53,54,55,56
John 8:31–42

APRIL 10

Jesus said to the Jews:
"Amen, amen, I say to you,
whoever keeps my word will never see death."
—JOHN 8:51

If we believe this statement of Jesus, then we accept a reality
that is quite beyond our understanding. We know that we
will die physically, but our connection to Jesus changes death
as we know it. Christian mystics might say that, at death, we
are united to Jesus as never before, and so death really has no
negative meaning. It has ceased to be something we need to
fear. This alone is a liberation, isn't it?

Genesis 17:3–9
Psalm 105:4–5,6–7,8–9
John 8:51–59

Friday

APRIL 11

• ST. STANISLAUS, BISHOP AND MARTYR •

The breakers of death surged round about me,
the destroying floods overwhelmed me;
The cords of the nether world enmeshed me,
the snares of death overtook me.
—PSALM 18:5–6

The psalms are poetry: they use imagery and drama to describe how the psalmist feels. Most of us have felt this way—as if we're drowning in worries, tangled up in troubles, coming close to death. We can make good use of this psalm and pray with it just as its author did. For centuries, Jews, Christians, and Muslims have used the book of Psalms to express the honest feelings of their hearts.

Jeremiah 20:10–13
Psalm 18:2–3a,3bc–4,5–6,7
John 10:31–42

"If we leave [Jesus] alone, all will believe in him,
and the Romans will come
and take away both our land and our nation."
—JOHN 11:48

The Sanhedrin worried about a real possibility. If Jesus
caused too much of a commotion, then no telling what the
occupying Roman forces would do to contain it. The Jewish
leaders chose safety for their people and land over the truth
of who Jesus was and what he taught. To be honest, I might
have made the same decision. What about you?

Ezekiel 37:21–28
Jeremiah 31:10,11–12abcd,13
John 11:45–56

Sunday

APRIL 13

• PALM SUNDAY OF THE PASSION OF THE LORD •

After withdrawing about a stone's throw from them and kneeling,
he prayed, saying, "Father, if you are willing,
take this cup away from me;
still, not my will but yours be done."
—LUKE 22:41–42

We must not forget this, ever. Jesus did not long for
martyrdom. He didn't get some macho thrill out of facing
down the authorities, then being publicly executed. He did
not want to go through any of this. Yet he discerned, over the
many months, weeks, and days prior to this moment, that
this was indeed the path ahead of him, the path on which the
Spirit led him, the path where the Father waited for him.
Lord Jesus, give me the strength to follow whatever path is
the right one for me.

PROCESSION:
Luke 19:28–40

MASS:
Isaiah 50:4–7
Psalm 22:8–9,17–18,19–20,23–24 (2a)
Philippians 2:6–11
Luke 22:14—23:56 or 23:1–49

*And the chief priests plotted to kill Lazarus too,
because many of the Jews were turning away
and believing in Jesus because of him.*
—JOHN 12:10–11

The plot of the chief priests has expanded; now they want to kill Lazarus, too, because his resurrection from death is yet more proof of Jesus' true identity as having been sent by God. Where will these people stop? At what point do you look at your plan and admit that its logical end is not a good one? Would they kill *more* people—those healed by Jesus, those he delivered from demons? I guess the real question is, What would it take to simply accept the truth? More to the point: What makes *me* resist the truth, and just how stubborn am I prepared to be?

Isaiah 42:1–7
Psalm 27:1,2,3,13–14
John 12:1–11

Tuesday

APRIL 15

• TUESDAY OF HOLY WEEK •

Though I thought I had toiled in vain,
and for nothing, uselessly, spent my strength,
Yet my reward is with the LORD,
my recompense is with my God.
—ISAIAH 49:4

The older I get, the more I aspire to the trait of spiritual freedom. I can make good plans, discern prayerfully what to do and when, and work hard and faithfully. But the outcome is out of my hands. Spiritual freedom enables me to let go of expectations, of clinging to one outcome over another. I do what I know to do but then leave the result to God. It's not for me to judge whether I've "toiled in vain, and for nothing." Whew! That's a responsibility I don't want anyway.

Isaiah 49:1–6
Psalm 71:1–2,3–4a,5ab–6ab,15 and 17
John 13:21–33,36–38

Wednesday

APRIL 16

I have become an outcast to my brothers,
a stranger to my mother's sons,
because zeal for your house consumes me,
and the insults of those who blaspheme you fall upon me.
—PSALM 69:9–10

Jesus accepted isolation, estrangement, and insults because
above all else—family and community—he valued and loved
the heavenly Father. Jesus understood that ultimate reality is
defined in that realm, whether we call it God's house or
kingdom or reign. When we align our lives with reality,
everything else will become reshaped and renewed.

Isaiah 50:4–9a
Psalm 69:8–10,21–22,31 and 33–34
Matthew 26:14–25

Thursday

APRIL 17

• THURSDAY OF HOLY WEEK (HOLY THURSDAY) •

He has sent me to bring glad tidings to the lowly,
to heal the brokenhearted,
To proclaim liberty to the captives
and release to the prisoners.
—ISAIAH 61:1

God who loves us, please show us how to give good news to
those who are down, bring healing to those who are broken,
and bring freedom to those who have been imprisoned.
Renew our sense of what is important to you, O Lord.

CHRISM MASS:
Isaiah 61:1–3a,6a,8b–9
Psalm 89:21–22,25,27
Revelation 1:5–8
Luke 4:16–21

EVENING MASS OF THE LORD'S SUPPER:
Exodus 12:1–8,11–14
Psalm 116:12–13,15–16bc,17–18
1 Corinthians 11:23–26
John 13:1–15

• FRIDAY OF THE PASSION OF THE LORD (GOOD FRIDAY) •

*Standing by the cross of Jesus were his mother
and his mother's sister, Mary the wife of Clopas,
and Mary of Magdala.*
—JOHN 19:25

On this blessed Friday of the Passion, we ask that God bring comfort and courage to women all over the world who must stand by and watch their loved ones being captured, tortured, killed. We ask God's mercy for the women who wait and pray for loved ones who have disappeared or who are in prison or who have been sent into war. God bestow grace on all the mothers, sisters, daughters, and friends who stay close, who do not leave or give up.

Isaiah 52:13—53:12
Psalm 31:2,6,12–13,15–16,17,25
Hebrews 4:14–16; 5:7–9
John 18:1—19:42

APRIL 19

Saturday

• HOLY SATURDAY •

*In the beginning, when God created the heavens and the earth,
the earth was a formless wasteland, and darkness covered the abyss,
while a mighty wind swept over the waters.*
—GENESIS 1:1–2

Holy Saturday is a day of silence, pondering, waiting,
grieving, and longing. The image of an unformed world,
darkness, and an abyss is quite appropriate. Then a wind
moves over the waters. On this day, God's Spirit is moving
over us, over the dark stillness of Holy Saturday.
Something is coming.

VIGIL:
Genesis 1:1—2:2 or 1:1,26–31a
Psalm 104:1–2,5–6,10,12,13–14,24,35 or
33:4–5,6–7,12–13,20–22
Genesis 22:1–18 or 22:1–2,9a,10–13,15–18
Psalm 16:5,8,9–10,11
Exodus 14:15—15:1
Exodus 15:1–2,3–4,5–6,17–18
Isaiah 54:5–14
Psalm 30:2,4,5–6,11–12,13 (2a)
Isaiah 55:1–11

Isaiah 12:2–3,4,5–6 (3)
Baruch 3:9–15,32—4:4
Psalm 19:8,9,10,11
Ezekiel 36:16–17a,18–28
Psalm 42:3,5; 43:3,4 or Isaiah
12:2–3,4bcd,5–6 or Psalm
51:12–13,14–15,18–19
Romans 6:3–11
Psalm 118:1–2,16–17,22–23
Luke 24:1–12

For our paschal lamb, Christ, has been sacrificed.
Therefore, let us celebrate the feast,
not with the old yeast, the yeast of malice and wickedness,
but with the unleavened bread of sincerity and truth.
—1 CORINTHIANS 5:7–8

Christ is risen! Our reality is transformed! May we live out this truth moment by moment and day by day. Through the power of the Resurrection, we can choose to live as the Christ lived. Indeed, the Resurrection is already at work within us, remaking us, birthing us to new life.

Acts 10:34a,37–43
Psalm 118:1–2,16–17,22–23 (24)
Colossians 3:1–4 or 1 Corinthians 5:6b–8
John 20:1–9 or Luke 24:1–12
Or, at an afternoon or evening Mass, Luke 24:13–35

Therefore my heart is glad and my soul rejoices,
my body, too, abides in confidence;
Because you will not abandon my soul to the nether world,
nor will you suffer your faithful one to undergo corruption.
—PSALM 16:9–10

These few words of the psalm include every aspect of being
human: heart, soul, and body. God will preserve it all. We are
whole persons who exist in the material and spiritual realms.
Therefore, we do well to honor the physical life as well as
the interior one. This day, entrust body and soul to
God's care.

Acts 2:14,22–33
Psalm 16:1–2a and 5,7–8,9–10,11
Matthew 28:8–15

⇒ 142 ⇐

Tuesday

APRIL 22

Mary Magdalene stayed outside the tomb weeping.
—JOHN 20:11

Mary stayed at the tomb of her friend and teacher. This is a hard place to inhabit, for any of us. The world tells us to "get on with your life." We're given a short time to grieve and then are pressured to stifle our tears and sorrow and look ahead. In this case, Mary had double reason to grieve, because Jesus' body was now missing. What more could possibly go wrong? Yet she lingered there, at the tomb of a criminal. And that's where Jesus met her. Let's give proper space to our emotions and adequate time to reflect and search. Jesus will meet us in that difficult place.

Acts 2:36–41
Psalm 33:4–5,18–19,20 and 22
John 20:11–18

"Were not our hearts burning within us
while he spoke to us on the way and opened the Scriptures to us?"
—LUKE 24:32

These two disciples on the road to Emmaus reflected on their
experience and did what we call discernment. They recalled
how they had felt while Jesus was speaking with them. They
noted something deep within themselves responding to this
man they did not yet recognize. You and I have had similar
experiences, when a distinct thought or sensation or intuition
alerted us to pay attention because something important was
happening. On what experience can you reflect today?

Acts 3:1–10
Psalm 105:1–2,3–4,6–7,8–9
Luke 24:13–35

Thursday

APRIL 24

• THURSDAY WITHIN THE OCTAVE OF EASTER •

"Repent, therefore, and be converted, that your sins may be wiped away,
and that the Lord may grant you times of refreshment
and send you the Christ already appointed for you, Jesus,
whom heaven must receive until the times of universal restoration
of which God spoke through the mouth
of his holy prophets from of old."
—ACTS 3:19–21

Peter is presenting an expansive view here, one that begins
with individual conversion and community conversion but
extends to a universal restoration. We are part of a grand,
eternal drama. And it's not over yet! May this increase our
hope in the meantime.

Acts 3:11–26
Psalm 8:2ab and 5,6–7,8–9
Luke 24:35–48

Jesus said to them, "Come, have breakfast."
And none of the disciples dared to ask him, "Who are you?"
because they realized it was the Lord.
—JOHN 21:12

A few of the disciples decided to go fishing, maybe for old
times' sake—it's what they'd done before they followed Jesus.
Jesus shows up on the shore, beside a cooking fire, when
they return. He shows up where he knows we'll be. When we
go about our daily business, in a good mood or a bad one,
full of faith or sorrow, Jesus finds us. We must remember this:
Jesus comes looking for us, ready to converse, ready to meet
our current need.

Acts 4:1–12
Psalm 118:1–2 and 4,22–24,25–27a
John 21:1–14

*"Whether it is right in the sight of God
for us to obey you rather than God, you be the judges.
It is impossible for us not to speak about what we have seen and heard."*
—ACTS 4:19

I don't believe that Jesus will scold us for the theology we
didn't quite get or tasks we didn't do perfectly. He may ask us
a pointed question, however: "How could you ignore what
was right in front of you?" The disciples had experienced
knowing Jesus and witnessing his works. Of these things they
were certain, and they could not contain the truth they'd
been given. What about us? Are we so concerned about
winning arguments or improving ourselves that we dismiss
the grace we have experienced in Christ Jesus?

Acts 4:13–21
Psalm 118:1 and 14–15ab,16–18,19–21
Mark 16:9–15

Sunday
APRIL 27

I, John, your brother, who share with you
the distress, the kingdom, and the endurance we have in Jesus,
found myself on the island called Patmos
because I proclaimed God's word and gave testimony to Jesus.
—REVELATION 1:9

John shares with his readers distress, the kingdom, and endurance. This is not a sunshiny opening for a letter to other Christians. John assumes that they, too, are in distress and must endure. Also, they experience themselves as belonging to the Christ community, the kingdom. We learn, too, that John is in exile because of his evangelism. Thus, the believers of this time assumed that following Jesus was a difficult path that could cost them their freedom, even their lives. How would you describe the Christian life?

Acts 5:12–16
Psalm 118:2–4,13–15,22–24
Revelation 1:9–11a,12–13,17–19
John 20:19–31

Monday

APRIL 28

• ST. PETER CHANEL, PRIEST AND MARTYR •
ST. LOUIS GRIGNION DE MONTFORT, PRIEST •

Nicodemus said to [Jesus],
"How can a man once grown old be born again?
Surely he cannot reenter his mother's womb and be born again, can he?"
—JOHN 3:4

Nicodemus has asked a logical question of Jesus. In this
passage, it appears that Nicodemus genuinely wants to
understand what Jesus is saying. But sometimes logic fails us.
Sometimes the questions we get stuck on are not really the
right questions. Jesus replies by referring to our inability to
know where the wind comes from or goes to. He is trying to
point Nicodemus to a deeper understanding, something
beyond mere reason. What questions have you asked
Jesus lately?

Acts 4:23–31
Psalm 2:1–3,4–7a,7b–9
John 3:1–8

⇒ 149 ⇐

The community of believers was of one heart and mind,
and no one claimed that any of his possessions was his own,
but they had everything in common.
—ACTS 4:32

We tend to read past this description of the believing
community in the book of Acts. It's quite radical to give up
private property and live in community. Some people would
call that communism or socialism and loudly protest how
anti-Christian it is. But we cannot deny this record of the
early church. What would it mean to become more like these
early believers? What aspects of our lives would it challenge?
Are we willing even to ask the question?

Acts 4:32–37
Psalm 93:1ab,1cd–2,5
John 3:7b–15

$\mathscr{W}ednesday$

APRIL 30

• ST. PIUS V, POPE •

Look to him that you may be radiant with joy,
and your faces may not blush with shame.
—PSALM 34:6

Where we focus our gaze determines so much about how we
live. Can I focus on the God who creates me and loves me,
on Jesus who blazed the trail of life and forgiveness, on the
Holy Spirit who accompanies and counsels me? If we're
lacking joy, perhaps it's time to refocus our attention.

Acts 5:17–26
Psalm 34:2–3,4–5,6–7,8–9
John 3:16–21

⇒ 151 ⇐

Thursday

MAY 1

• ST. JOSEPH THE WORKER •

The one who comes from above is above all.
The one who is of the earth is earthly and speaks of earthly things.
—JOHN 3:31

We are reminded here that there's a vast difference between
those who dwell in this material world of time and space and
those who dwell in the realm of mystery. When we cannot
make sense of faith, when we do not understand God's action
or what we perceive as inaction, we can recall these simple
statements from John's Gospel and perhaps take a deep
breath and grow more patient.

Acts 5:27–33
Psalm 34:2 and 9,17–18,19–20
John 3:31–36
Or, for the Optional Memorial, Genesis 1:26—2:3 or
Colossians 3:14–15, 17, 23–24 / Matthew 13:54–58

Friday

MAY 2

Since Jesus knew that they were going to come and carry him off
to make him king,
he withdrew again to the mountain alone.

—JOHN 6:15

It takes a wise and grounded person to resist being carried off
by strong public opinion, especially when the public heaps
praise upon that person, freely giving him power. Can you
imagine how good Jesus felt to see people welcoming him,
listening to him, responding positively to his message? Had
he not known better, this wonderful feeling could have
convinced him to simply go with the flow of these joyful
moments. But he practiced true discernment, constantly
attending to God's voice in his mind and heart.

Acts 5:34–42
Psalm 27:1,4,13–14
John 6:1–15

[Jesus said,] "The words that I speak to you I do not speak on my own. The Father who dwells in me is doing his works."
—JOHN 14:10

This is how we are to imitate Jesus: listen to the Father, look to the Father, remain in communion always with the Father. As we learn to live this way, we will speak what God is speaking, and God's works will be manifested in us.

1 Corinthians 15:1–8
Psalm 19:2–3,4–5
John 14:6–14

Sunday

MAY 4

• THIRD SUNDAY OF EASTER •

When they had finished breakfast, Jesus said to Simon Peter,
"Simon, son of John, do you love me more than these?"
Simon Peter answered him, "Yes, Lord, you know that I love you."
Jesus said to him, "Feed my lambs."
—JOHN 21:15

Lord, today I say that I love you. Where are the lambs that I
must feed? Who needs help, acceptance, a person to be safe
with, a hopeful word? Open my eyes to see your lambs.

Acts 5:27–32,40b–41
Psalm 30:2,4,5–6,11–12,13 (2a)
5:11–14
John 21:1–19 or Revelation 21:1–14

Monday

MAY 5

Jesus answered them and said,
"Amen, amen, I say to you, you are looking for me
not because you saw signs
but because you ate the loaves and were filled."
—JOHN 6:26

I don't think Jesus was scolding the people for their motives,
but he was voicing his observation. This gave them the
opportunity to ask more questions and learn more from him.
May we be open when the Holy Spirit challenges us; may it
spur us to deeper questions and, ultimately, more maturity.

Acts 6:8–15
Psalm 119:23–24,26–27,29–30
John 6:22–29

⇒ 156 ⇐

Tuesday

MAY 6

Into your hands I commend my spirit;
you will redeem me, O LORD, O faithful God.
My trust is in the LORD;
I will rejoice and be glad of your mercy.
—PSALM 31:6–8

Jesus quoted this psalm just before he died on the cross. And
when Stephen was about to be martyred, he said, "Lord Jesus,
receive my spirit." We, too, can murmur this psalm as a
prayer when we are in a desperate situation, when we are
oppressed by fear or pain, when we believe that the end is
near. Scripture is given to us for many reasons. Let us not
hesitate to turn to sacred words for comfort and hope.

Acts 7:51—8:1a
Psalm 31:3cd–4,6 and 7b and 8a,17 and 21ab
John 6:30–35

Wednesday

MAY 7

Jesus said to the crowds,
"I am the bread of life;
whoever comes to me will never hunger,
and whoever believes in me will never thirst."
—JOHN 6:35

What kind of hunger and thirst is Jesus talking about here? Does he refer to our simple needs for daily sustenance? Does he mean that, after believing in him, we will no longer experience desire or lack of any kind? Perhaps it's more fruitful to meditate on these questions: What hunger within me refuses to be satisfied by anything but Jesus' companionship? What thirst leads me to the most fundamental desire within me, the desire planted there so that I might seek beyond everything else until I encounter God?

Acts 8:1b–8
Psalm 66:1–3a,4–5,6–7a
John 6:35–40

MAY 8

The angel of the Lord spoke to Philip,
"Get up and head south on the road
that goes down from Jerusalem to Gaza, the desert route."
So he got up and set out.
—ACTS 8:26–27A

It's not uncommon to hear of someone being awakened in the early hours of the morning and feeling compelled to pray for a specific person—and learning later that, at that very moment, that person was in dire need. Or to feel an inner nudge to speak to someone or change a plan. This is not magic or extrasensory perception. These moments are holy invitations. But we must live in a posture of readiness, openness, even adventure.

Acts 8:26–40
Psalm 66:8–9,16–17,20
John 6:44–51

Ananias went and entered the house;
laying his hands on him, he said,
"Saul, my brother, the Lord has sent me,
Jesus who appeared to you on the way by which you came,
that you may regain your sight and be filled with the Holy Spirit."
—ACTS 9:17

This scene is almost comical, in that the Lord told Ananias to go to Saul and pray for him, and Ananias knew that Saul was a dangerous man to the Jesus community. But God had *already* given Saul a vision of Ananias coming to see him! I imagine Ananias's hands shaking just a bit when he laid them on Saul and called the man "brother." Both men, one a believer and one not, heard from God and did what they were told. Thus began a whole new chapter in the early church.

Acts 9:1–20
Psalm 117:1bc,2
John 6:52–59

Saturday

MAY 10

• ST. DAMIEN DE VEUSTER, PRIEST •

The Church throughout all Judea, Galilee, and Samaria was at peace.
She was being built up and walked in the fear of the Lord,
and with the consolation of the Holy Spirit she grew in numbers.
—ACTS 9:31

Dear Holy Spirit, please bring about the fruit in today's
church that was so evident back in the early days. May we be
at peace, walk in the fear of the Lord, and, in the consolation
of the Holy Spirit, grow and mature.

Acts 9:31–42
Psalm 116:12–13,14–15,16–17
John 6:60–69

⇒ 161 ⇐

Sunday

MAY 11

• FOURTH SUNDAY OF EASTER •

I, John, had a vision of a great multitude,
which no one could count,
from every nation, race, people, and tongue.
They stood before the throne and before the Lamb,
wearing white robes and holding palm branches in their hands.
—REVELATION 7:9

John gives us a hopeful, majestic vision of who we are and who we are becoming: the people of God, innumerable, from every place and time, together in joy, at last in that far home, which is God's presence, Jesus at our center. When, in the present, we grow weary of trials and the church's imperfections, we can hold this vision in prayer and gratitude.

Acts 13:14,43–52
Psalm 100:1–2,3,5 (3c)
Revelation 7:9,14b–17
John 10:27–30

• ST. NEREUS AND ST. ACHILLEUS, MARTYRS • ST. PANCRAS, MARTYR •

[Peter said,] "If then God gave them the same gift he gave to us
when we came to believe in the Lord Jesus Christ,
who was I to be able to hinder God?"
When they heard this,
they stopped objecting and glorified God, saying,
"God has then granted life-giving repentance to the Gentiles too."
—ACTS 11:17–18

We must pay attention, brothers and sisters, to the evidence
in front of us, when God appears in the lives of others. We
may not understand it, but God will show us how much he
loves people despite our biases and expectations.

Acts 11:1–18
Psalm 42:2–3; 43:3,4
John 10:1–10

Tuesday

MAY 13

• OUR LADY OF FATIMA •

[Jesus said,] "My sheep hear my voice,
I know them, and they follow me.
I give them eternal life, and they shall never perish.
No one can take them out of my hand."
—JOHN 10:27–28

Here is our security. We belong to Jesus,
and no one can take us from him.

Acts 11:19–26
Psalm 87:1b–3,4–5,6–7
John 10:22–30

Wednesday

MAY 14

Then they gave lots to them, and the lot fell upon Matthias,
and he was counted with the eleven apostles.
—ACTS 1:26

Today, let us pray for every man and woman like Matthias,
who, after much quiet, faithful service to God's kingdom, is
chosen for even more responsibility, and sometimes a higher
profile. We never know when the Holy Spirit will choose us
for such a position, but may we not hold back when that
happens. Then it's time to own our gifts and our calling and
move forward with spiritual confidence.

Acts 1:15–17,20–26
Psalm 113:1–2,3–4,5–6,7–8
John 15:9–17

Thursday

MAY 15

When Jesus had washed the disciples' feet, he said to them:
"Amen, amen, I say to you, no slave is greater than his master
nor any messenger greater than the one who sent him."
—JOHN 13:16

What exactly is Jesus saying? Perhaps it's simply this: "Your
task is to imitate me, even to the point of acting like a
servant, washing others' feet." He knew that the systems of
power and domination would tempt the disciples to interact
with others through pride, cajoling, and manipulation. But he
was showing them the truest way: serving others as he had
served them. In your life today, what would servanthood
look like?

Acts 13:13–25
Psalm 89:2–3,21–22,25 and 27
John 13:16–20

Friday

MAY 16

Jesus said to his disciples:
"Do not let your hearts be troubled.
You have faith in God; have faith also in me.
In my Father's house there are many dwelling places.
If there were not,
would I have told you that I am going to prepare a place for you?
And if I go and prepare a place for you,
I will come back again and take you to myself,
so that where I am you also may be."
—JOHN 14:1–3

Sometimes, here in this life, we are troubled, even to the point of despair. These words of Jesus can become our mantra during such periods. Why not make a little poster out of them and hang it prominently in your home?

Acts 13:26–33
Psalm 2:6–7,8–9,10–11ab
John 14:1–6

Saturday

MAY 17

*Jesus said to him, "Have I been with you for so long a time
and you still do not know me, Philip?
Whoever has seen me has seen the Father."*
—JOHN 14:9

It is quite unbelievable that God of the Universe would show
up as a human being among us. Yet Jesus says clearly that
whoever has seen him has also seen the Father. Through the
centuries, people have stumbled over the idea that a human
being could also be divine—or that the divine could come to
us in human form. But this is a fundamental tenet of the
Christian faith. We do well to meditate on this paradox and
send our questions to God.

Acts 13:44–52
Psalm 98:1,2–3ab,3cd–4
John 14:7–14

≥ 168 ≤

Sunday

MAY 18

• FIFTH SUNDAY OF EASTER •

I heard a loud voice from the throne saying,
"Behold, God's dwelling is with the human race.
He will dwell with them and they will be his people
and God himself will always be with them as their God."
—REVELATION 21:3

How can we read this passage and not be overwhelmed with
joy and relief? God has chosen to dwell with us! God has
said, "You belong to me, and I belong to you." What more
could we ever want or need?

Acts 14:21–27
Psalm 145:8–9,10–11,12–13
Revelation 21:1–5a
John 13:31–33a,34–35

———————

Monday

MAY 19

When the crowds saw what Paul had done,
they cried out in Lycaonian,
"The gods have come down to us in human form."
They called Barnabas "Zeus" and Paul "Hermes,"
because he was the chief speaker.
—ACTS 14:11-12

After Paul healed a man, the crowds responded in the only way they knew: they gave to Paul and Barnabas the names of gods they had heard of. When we share the good news of Jesus with others, we must be sensitive to how a person sees the world and what names and terms he or she knows already. He may have an authentic experience with God but call it something else. She may be able to speak of her spiritual life only in psychological terms. Such conversations require patience and trust in the Holy Spirit to guide people into new knowledge.

Acts 14:5–18
Psalm 115:1–2,3–4,15–16
John 14:21–26

*[Paul and Barnabas] strengthened the spirits of the disciples
and exhorted them to persevere in the faith, saying,
"It is necessary for us to undergo many hardships
to enter the Kingdom of God."*
—ACTS 14:22

Most people know the truth: life is hard. When someone
tries to gloss over the truth with pious sayings, the listeners
stop listening. Rather than promise people that God will
protect them always and keep bad things from happening, it
would be better to say, "Spiritual growth and integrity have
always been hard-won through trials and suffering."
Certainly the early Christians knew this. When did we mix
up this message?

Acts 14:19–28
Psalm 145:10–11,12–13ab,21
John 14:27–31a

Wednesday

MAY 21

• ST. CHRISTOPHER MAGALLANES, PRIEST, AND COMPANIONS, MARTYRS •

Because there arose no little dissension and debate
by Paul and Barnabas with them,
it was decided that Paul, Barnabas, and some of the others
should go up to Jerusalem to the Apostles and presbyters
about this question.
—ACTS 15:2

It's important to note that leaders in the church could not
come to agreement. Rather than fracture the church, these
leaders traveled to Jerusalem to meet with other leaders.
They understood that the Holy Spirit could work within
their communion and help them discern the best way to
proceed. Sometimes, an individual's prayers are insufficient,
even if that individual has a close relationship with God. God
designed us, the Body of Christ, to function in community.

Acts 15:1–6
Psalm 122:1–2,3–4ab,4cd–5
John 15:1–8

Thursday

MAY 22

• ST. RITA OF CASCIA, RELIGIOUS •

"[God] made no distinction between us and them,
for by faith he purified their hearts.
Why, then, are you now putting God to the test
by placing on the shoulders of the disciples
a yoke that neither our ancestors nor we have been able to bear?"
—ACTS 15:9–10

The apostle Peter exhorts the council to refrain from laying
upon non-Jewish believers the many rules of Judaism,
because people are saved by faith in Jesus. You might say that
Peter is thinking like a pastor here. If God draws non-Jews
into the Jesus community, then why should the Jews make
this new life of faith overly difficult for them? I have to ask:
Do I ever make the Christian life difficult for others?

Acts 15:7–21
Psalm 96:1–2a,2b–3,10
John 15:9–11

Friday

MAY 23

"I no longer call you slaves,
because a slave does not know what his master is doing.
I have called you friends,
because I have told you everything I have heard from my Father."
—JOHN 15:15

If you truly believed, here and now, that God longs for your
friendship, how might that change the way you go
through today?

Acts 15:22–31
Psalm 57:8–9,10 and 12
John 15:12–17

*When they came to Mysia, they tried to go on into Bithynia,
but the Spirit of Jesus did not allow them,
so they crossed through Mysia and came down to Troas.*
—ACTS 16:7–8

I admire Paul and his companions for planning to spread the
news of Jesus everywhere they went. They would finish in
one town and push on to the next. Can you imagine the
spiritual courage they had? Still, courage must be balanced
with wisdom. One or more of them understood that Jesus
was preventing their entry to Bithynia. No doubt they
discussed this and prayed together. Then they changed their
plans. Courage and discernment—a powerful combination!

Acts 16:1–10
Psalm 100:1b–2,3,5
John 15:18–21

Sunday

MAY 25

• SIXTH SUNDAY OF EASTER •

[Jesus said,] "The Advocate, the Holy Spirit,
whom the Father will send in my name,
will teach you everything
and remind you of all that I told you."
—JOHN 14:26

If the Holy Spirit would teach Jesus' disciples everything, then it seems that there was still something to learn. Not only that, but the Spirit would remind them of what they already knew because Jesus had told them. So, we can expect to keep learning. We can also rely on the Holy Spirit to remind us of what we have already learned. We are still in process. We have no excuse to remain complacent or inactive.

Acts 15:1–2,22–29
Psalm 67:2–3,5,6,8 (4)
Revelation 21:10–14,22–23
John 14:23–29

One of them, a woman named Lydia, a dealer in purple cloth,
from the city of Thyatira, a worshiper of God, listened,
and the Lord opened her heart to pay attention
to what Paul was saying.
—ACTS 16:14

Paul went looking for people gathered in prayer and found a group of women. So he spoke with them. Lydia was drawn to pay attention to Paul's words. So often, this is how evangelism happens: we talk with whomever we encounter, and a person's heart opens, and the conversion begins. Let's not discount our everyday encounters and conversations. We never know whom Jesus has prepared to hear the Good News.

Acts 16:11–15
Psalm 149:1b–2,3–4,5–6a and 9b
John 15:26—16:4a

Tuesday

MAY 27

Jesus said to his disciples,
"Now I am going to the one who sent me,
and not one of you asks me, 'Where are you going?'
But because I told you this, grief has filled your hearts."
—JOHN 16:5–6

Jesus understands that even this close to the end of his
ministry, his disciples struggle to understand him and his
mission. He knows they are afraid to ask questions. He
knows that his various predictions of his violent end have
upset them. Here, he brings their struggle out in the open. If
we stay with Jesus, continue to follow him, and try to
believe, then he will help us over the rough spots.

Acts 16:22–34
Psalm 138:1–2ab,2cde–3,7c–8
John 16:5–11

Jesus said to his disciples,
"I have much more to tell you, but you cannot bear it now.
But when he comes, the Spirit of truth,
he will guide you to all truth."
—JOHN 16:12–13

It's interesting to me that, despite these words of Jesus, we resist learning anything new, as if the Holy Spirit led people into the truth only during the first couple of centuries but not anymore. Jesus knew only what he heard from the Father; I doubt he could see ahead to the unfolding of history and the discovery of electricity or psychology or quantum physics. But he was confident that the Spirit would remain with us and continue revealing truth. Are *we* confident in the Spirit to do this?

Acts 17:15,22—18:1
Psalm 148:1–2,11–12,13,14
John 16:12–15

Thursday

MAY 29

[Jesus said,] "Amen, amen, I say to you,
you will weep and mourn, while the world rejoices;
you will grieve, but your grief will become joy."
—JOHN 16:20

While the world rejoices—while Jesus' enemies shout in
victory as he is put to death on a Roman cross—the disciples
will weep and mourn. This cannot be avoided. Jesus knows
that they do not yet understand what all of this means. So,
he tries to prepare them for what's ahead. He also voices the
hope of resurrection, the grief that will become joy. Of
course they don't see it yet. But when the impossible
happens, they will remember what he said.

Acts 18:1–8
Psalm 98:1,2–3ab,3cd–4
John 16:16–20
For the Ecclesiastical Provinces of Boston, Hartford, New York, Omaha, Philadelphia:
The Ascension of the Lord: Acts 1:1–11 / Psalm 47:2–3,6–7,8–9 (6) / Ephesians 1:17–23 or
Hebrews 9:24–28; 10:19–23 / Luke 24:46–53

One night while Paul was in Corinth, the Lord said to him in a vision,
"Do not be afraid.
Go on speaking, and do not be silent, for I am with you.
No one will attack and harm you,
for I have many people in this city."
He settled there for a year and a half
and taught the word of God among them.
—ACTS 18:9–11

God prepares a way for us. Sometimes that way includes trouble and trial, but not always. Paul enjoyed a peaceful year and a half in which to teach the believers in Corinth. We can thank God for the peaceful way, and for times of calm.

Acts 18:9–18
Psalm 47:2–3,4–5,6–7
John 16:20–23

Saturday

MAY 31

• THE VISITATION OF THE BLESSED VIRGIN MARY •

God indeed is my savior;
I am confident and unafraid.
My strength and my courage is the LORD,
and he has been my savior.
With joy you will draw water
at the fountain of salvation.
—ISAIAH 12:2–3

We might wonder at Mary's quick willingness to say yes to God's plan for her. But she had grown up hearing Scriptures such as this passage in Isaiah. Perhaps she had even memorized it. She had been learning to have faith up until this crucial moment. God prepares us, too, for our moments of decision.

Zephaniah 3:14–18a or Romans 12:9–16
Isaiah 12:2–3,4bcd,5–6
Luke 1:39–56

Sunday

JUNE 1

• THE ASCENSION OF THE LORD •

As he blessed them he parted from them
and was taken up to heaven.
They did him homage
and then returned to Jerusalem with great joy,
and they were continually in the temple praising God.
—LUKE 24:51–53

Jesus has just left his disciples, to reside with the Father. The
Holy Spirit has not yet descended. Still, they are full of joy
and worship! This is the work of faith. They truly believe
now what Jesus has told them. This faith has taken hold, and
they are different people now—full of joy rather than fear
and sorrow. Faith is given us for many reasons; may we not
forget that one of those reasons is joy.

Acts 1:1–11
Psalm 47:2–3,6–7,8–9 (6)
Hebrews 9:24–28; 10:19–23 or Ephesians 1:17–23
Luke 24:46–53
Or, for the Ecclesiastical Provinces of Boston, Hartford, New York, Omaha, and
Philadelphia, readings for the Seventh Sunday of Easter: Acts 7:55–60 / Revelation
22:12–14,16–17, 20 / John 17:20–26

Monday

JUNE 2

• ST. MARCELLINUS AND ST. PETER, MARTYRS •

The father of orphans and the defender of widows
is God in his holy dwelling.
God gives a home to the forsaken;
he leads forth prisoners to prosperity.
—PSALM 68:6–7

When you see orphans, widows, the homeless, and the imprisoned helped, it's safe to assume that God is in that activity. Pay attention to those who do what God desires.

Acts 19:1–8
Psalm 68:2–3ab,4–5acd,6–7ab
John 16:29–33

Tuesday

JUNE 3

• ST. CHARLES LWANGA AND COMPANIONS, MARTYRS •

"Now this is eternal life,
that they should know you, the only true God,
and the one whom you sent, Jesus Christ."
—JOHN 17:3

Jesus doesn't say here that eternal life is living forever; he
says that eternal life is knowing God and God's Son. Eternal
life is a relationship, not a destination. Do I desire eternal life
because I want to know God more and more, or because I
want to "go to heaven" when I die?

Acts 20:17–27
Psalm 68:10–11,20–21
John 17:1–11a

Lifting up his eyes to heaven, Jesus prayed, saying:
"Holy Father, keep them in your name
that you have given me,
so that they may be one just as we are one."
—JOHN 17:11B

Jesus' vision of what we call the Church is simply this: in the
same way Jesus dwells in perfect union with the Father, all of
us will live in perfect union with the Father, with Jesus, with
the Holy Spirit, and with one another. He does not paint a
picture of paradise, because the paradise is God's presence.
He does not describe what we will do or what we'll look like,
because those things are beside the point. We will dwell with
God—what more could we desire?

Acts 20:28–38
Psalm 68:29–30,33–35a,35bc–36ab
John 17:11b–19

Thursday

JUNE 5

• ST. BONIFACE, BISHOP AND MARTYR •

Lifting up his eyes to heaven, Jesus prayed, saying,
"I pray not only for these,
but also for those who will believe in me through their word,
so that they may all be one,
as you, Father, are in me and I in you,
that they also may be in us,
that the world may believe that you sent me."
—JOHN 17:20–21

We can read the whole of Jesus' prayer in John 17—and
apply it to us. He prayed for us in advance. We should read
this prayer often, don't you think?

Acts 22:30; 23:6–11
Psalm 16:1–2a and 5,7–8,9–10,11
John 17:20–26

Friday

JUNE 6

• ST. NORBERT, BISHOP •

For as the heavens are high above the earth,
so surpassing is his kindness toward those who fear him.
As far as the east is from the west,
so far has he put our transgressions from us.
—PSALM 103:11–12

When we turn to God for forgiveness and a new start, this is
what God does: he removes our sin absolutely. As members
of Christ's Body, we are not seen in light of the past or even
in light of our current struggles and growth. We are already
considered new and clean. Now, if only we could see
ourselves that way.

Acts 25:13b–21
Psalm 103:1–2,11–12,19–20ab
John 21:15–19

When he entered Rome, Paul was allowed to live by himself,
with the soldier who was guarding him. . . .
He remained for two full years in his lodgings.
He received all who came to him, and with complete assurance
and without hindrance he proclaimed the Kingdom of God
and taught about the Lord Jesus Christ.
—ACTS 28:16, 30–31

This is the apostle Paul under house arrest in Rome! As a prisoner, he was safe from enemies. He also could receive visitors and teach about Jesus without any disruption. Sometimes our trials turn into opportunities. Can you remember such a time in your life?

Acts 28:16–20,30–31
Psalm 11:4,5 and 7
John 21:20–25

Sunday

JUNE 8

• PENTECOST SUNDAY •

The hand of the LORD came upon me,
and he led me out in the spirit of the LORD
and set me in the center of the plain,
which was now filled with bones.
He made me walk among the bones in every direction
so that I saw how many they were on the surface of the plain.
—EZEKIEL 37:1–2

Before Ezekiel witnessed the valley of dry bones coming to life, he had to walk among them and experience the desolation. Sometimes God leads us into a place of death and dryness, perhaps so that we perceive just how desperate we are for life.

VIGIL:
Genesis 11:1–9 or Exodus 19:3–8a,16–20b
or Ezekiel 37:1–14 or Joel 3:1–5
Psalm 104:1–2,24,35,27–28,29,30
Romans 8:22–27
John 7:37–39

DAY:
Acts 2:1–11
Psalm 104:1,24,29–30,31,34
1 Corinthians 12:3b–7,12–13 or Romans
8:8–17
John 20:19–23 or 14:15–16,23b–26
Or, for the Extended Vigil: Genesis 11:1–9 /
Exodus 19:3–8a, 16–20b / Ezekiel 37:1–14 /
Joel 3:1–5 / Romans 8:22–27 / John 7:37–39

All these devoted themselves with one accord to prayer,
together with some women,
and Mary the mother of Jesus, and his brothers.
—ACTS 1:14

Mary, the mother of Jesus, was part of the believing
community. She was among the disciples. As a young girl,
she had said yes to God and carried Jesus in her womb. Now,
as an older woman, she said yes once again, to follow where
the Spirit was leading. We can suppose that, long ago, she
gave up any personal dreams of how her son's life would play
out. She knew that God's plans were beyond anyone's
imagination. We can look to her as an example
of discipleship.

Genesis 3:9–15,20 or Acts 1:12–14
Psalm 87:1–2,3 and 5,6–7
John 19:25–34

Tuesday

JUNE 10

> [Jesus said,] "Just so, your light must shine before others,
> that they may see your good deeds
> and glorify your heavenly Father."
> —MATTHEW 5:16

False modesty really gets in the way of people owning their faith and their gifts. Jesus is saying, "You're a light—so shine!" Whatever abilities or spiritual capacities we are given are meant to be worked to their fullest, and we can shine our light without being egotistical about it. When others see our gratitude toward God, when they hear us speak of our freedom in Christ, they will begin to look Godward.

2 Corinthians 1:18–22
Psalm 119:129,130,131,132,133,135
Matthew 5:13–16

Wednesday

JUNE 11

When [Barnabas] arrived and saw the grace of God,
he rejoiced and encouraged them all
to remain faithful to the Lord in firmness of heart,
for he was a good man, filled with the Holy Spirit and faith.
—ACTS 11:23–24

Barnabas was sent to Antioch; eventually he and Saul worked with the believers there for a year. We can imagine Barnabas's character: affirming, encouraging, hopeful. We don't know if he was a great speaker or teacher, but sometimes people learn more from character than from anything else. Whatever our gifts, we can always encourage others.

Acts 11:21b–26; 13:1–3
Psalm 98:1,2–3ab,3cd–4,5–6
Matthew 5:17–19

⇒ 193 ⇐

All of us, gazing with unveiled face on the glory of the Lord,
are being transformed into the same image from glory to glory,
as from the Lord who is the Spirit.
—2 CORINTHIANS 3:18

The Eastern as well as the Western Church use the terms
theosis and *divinization*. Both refer to the process by which
humans are transformed more and more into the likeness and
character of Christ. St. Athanasius said it like this: "God
became man so that man might become God." We don't talk
about this much, yet transformation is at the heart of our
faith. Will we believe this? Will we live in the light of
this truth?

2 Corinthians 3:15—4:1,3–6
Psalm 85:9ab and 10,11–12,13–14
Matthew 5:20–26

We are afflicted in every way, but not constrained;
perplexed, but not driven to despair;
persecuted, but not abandoned;
struck down, but not destroyed;
always carrying about in the body the dying of Jesus,
so that the life of Jesus may also be manifested in our body.
—2 CORINTHIANS 4:8–10

Now that we are part of the Body of Christ, we can view life in a new way. Our sufferings will never be the end of our story. In fact, our suffering allows us to share in Christ's suffering. Which means that we also share in his resurrection and life. All of this is a mystery, but we can believe it and count on it.

2 Corinthians 4:7–15
Psalm 116:10–11,15–16,17–18
Matthew 5:27–32

JUNE 14

So we are ambassadors for Christ,
as if God were appealing through us.
—2 CORINTHIANS 5:20A

Because I become irritated by other drivers, I have not put "Christian" bumper stickers on my car. The best solution is to learn not to become irritated. But in the meantime, I don't want my anger to represent Christ, even if the other driver is at fault! Dare I consider myself God's ambassador all day long, in every interaction with others?

2 Corinthians 5:14–21
Psalm 103:1–2,3–4,9–10,11–12
Matthew 5:33–37

We even boast of our afflictions,
knowing that affliction produces endurance,
and endurance, proven character,
and proven character, hope,
and hope does not disappoint,
because the love of God has been poured out into our hearts
through the Holy Spirit that has been given to us.
—ROMANS 5:3–5

First of all, this passage makes it clear that God does not always protect us from afflictions. Second, even they can be transformed through the power of the Holy Spirit. Perhaps, during hard times, we can pray, "Holy Spirit, work through this to accomplish God's purpose."

Proverbs 8:22–31
Psalm 8:4–5,6–7,8–9 (2a)
Romans 5:1–5
John 16:12–15

Jesus said to his disciples,
"You have heard that it was said,
An eye for an eye and a tooth for a tooth.
But I say to you, offer no resistance to one who is evil."
—MATTHEW 5:38–39

This teaching would certainly not be popular today in much of the United States, where so many people feel it necessary to carry guns, and where "stand your ground" laws justify a killing if the homeowner feels threatened enough. What was Jesus getting at? "An eye for an eye" referred to Old Testament laws limiting vengeance. But it seems that no vengeance is allowable in Jesus' view. No resistance. Sometimes Jesus seems quite unreasonable.

2 Corinthians 6:1–10
Psalm 98:1,2b,3ab,3cd–4
Matthew 5:38–42

*[Jesus said,] "But I say to you, love your enemies,
and pray for those who persecute you,
that you may be children of your heavenly Father,
for he makes his sun rise on the bad and the good
and causes rain to fall on the just and the unjust."*
—MATTHEW 5:44–45

Well, this is how Jesus wants us to respond to those who do evil. Yesterday we learned that he says not to resist them. Today he tells us to love them and pray for them. What a hard teaching to follow, when everything in us demands payback and punishment for those who do wrong. Jesus, give us the strength and wisdom to follow your holy and difficult way.

2 Corinthians 8:1–9
Psalm 146:2,5–6ab,6c–7,8–9a
Matthew 5:43–48

Wednesday
JUNE 18

The one who supplies seed to the sower and bread for food
will supply and multiply your seed
and increase the harvest of your righteousness.
—2 CORINTHIANS 9:10

It's encouraging to know that we are not responsible for the results of our work. As we follow the way of Jesus, which can be quite difficult sometimes, we simply do as the Spirit leads. Then we must let it all go and trust God to nurture what we have planted.

2 Corinthians 9:6–11
Psalm 112:1bc–2,3–4,9
Matthew 6:1–6,16–18

Thursday

JUNE 19

• ST. ROMUALD, ABBOT •

Jesus said to his disciples,
"In praying, do not babble like the pagans,
who think that they will be heard because of their many words."
—MATTHEW 6:7

I think that words make us feel powerful. We use them to persuade, to argue, to make our case, to explain ourselves. We are so accustomed to using words for these reasons in the world of people that we forget there's no need to persuade God or make our case before God. No need to explain ourselves either. Maybe more of our prayer should simply be silence in which we listen for what God might be saying to us.

2 Corinthians 11:1–11
Psalm 111:1b–2,3–4,7–8
Matthew 6:7–15

Friday

JUNE 20

*[Jesus said,] "The lamp of the body is the eye.
If your eye is sound, your whole body will be filled with light;
but if your eye is bad, your whole body will be in darkness."*
—MATTHEW 6:22–23

Light often means righteousness or spiritual wisdom. If our eye—our focus, our outlook—is healthy, then it will shed light, or wisdom, on what we see. Jesus is asking us to take responsibility for how we see. We can choose to look upon what is good and true. We can see the world with his compassion. We can look for what is wise and just. We do have a choice.

2 Corinthians 11:18,21–30
Psalm 34:2–3,4–5,6–7
Matthew 6:19–23

Saturday

JUNE 21

• ST. ALOYSIUS GONZAGA, RELIGIOUS •

*[Jesus said,] "So do not worry and say, 'What are we to eat?'
or 'What are we to drink?' or 'What are we to wear?'
All these things the pagans seek.
Your heavenly Father knows that you need them all."*
—MATTHEW 6:31–32

When you consider that Jesus was not speaking to wealthy
people, these words are quite challenging. In that time and
place, most of what people did was work so that they could
eat and clothe themselves. Jesus was inviting them to an
outlandish kind of faith. What is our response when Jesus
invites us to faith that seems impossible?

2 Corinthians 12:1–10
Psalm 34:8–9,10–11,12–13
Matthew 6:24–34

They all ate and were satisfied.
And when the leftover fragments were picked up,
they filled twelve wicker baskets.
—LUKE 9:17

Jesus has just fed thousands of people with five loaves and
two fish. After everyone finished, they gathered twelve
baskets of leftovers. When Jesus feeds us, there is abundance.
Just as his body and blood provide abundant resources for us.
This great feast gives us a picture of God's bounty and of
Jesus' generosity.

Genesis 14:18–20
Psalm 110:1,2,3,4 (4b)
1 Corinthians 11:23–26
Luke 9:11b–17

*[Jesus said,] "Why do you notice the splinter in your brother's eye,
but do not perceive the wooden beam in your own eye?"*
—MATTHEW 7:3

The science of psychology has revealed that what I notice
and dislike in other people is most likely a trait or behavior
in my own life. It is easier to judge it in someone else than
face it in myself. Jesus knew that judgmentalism is rooted in a
person's own sin and that no good comes from passing
judgment on others. This calls for a new habit: when I am
tempted to judge someone, I must look at myself.

Genesis 12:1–9
Psalm 33:12–13,18–19,20 and 22
Matthew 7:1–5

Tuesday

JUNE 24

• THE NATIVITY OF ST. JOHN THE BAPTIST •

"He will be filled with the Holy Spirit even from his mother's womb,
and he will turn many of the children of Israel
to the Lord their God."
—LUKE 1:15–16

So many people played a part in the coming of Jesus. Any
one of them could have resisted God's call. John the Baptist
could have turned his tremendous energy to other pursuits.
But it seems that his very birth set him on the path of a
prophet, the one who would prepare people to meet Jesus.
Each of us has a calling; what is yours? What part are you
asked to play in the grand drama of God's love?

VIGIL:
Jeremiah 1:4–10
Psalm 71:1–2,3–4a,5–6ab,15ab and 17
1 Peter 1:8–12
Luke 1:5–17

DAY:
Isaiah 49:1–6
Psalm 139:1b–3,13–14ab,14c–15
Acts 13:22–26
Luke 1:57–66,80

Jesus said to his disciples,
"Beware of false prophets, who come to you in sheep's clothing,
but underneath are ravenous wolves.
By their fruits you will know them."
—MATTHEW 7:15–16A

As a college student, I attended a seminar that was quite popular at the time. After a while, I felt uncomfortable with the teachings and stopped attending. Years later it was revealed that this ministry had done much damage to churches and families. What we might call bad fruit. We can assess whether a person or an organization is bearing good fruit. It's important to use discernment.

Genesis 15:1–12,17–18
Psalm 105:1–2,3–4,6–7,8–9
Matthew 7:15–20

Thursday

JUNE 26

Sarai said to Abram:
"The LORD has kept me from bearing children.
Have intercourse, then, with my maid;
perhaps I shall have sons through her."
Abram heeded Sarai's request.
—GENESIS 16:2

You could say that Sarai was resourceful, proactive, a problem solver. As it turned out, she and Abram did not wait for God to do as God had promised. Their solution resulted in conflict and complication. How important it is for us to learn discernment: how to listen to God and perceive what solutions are God's, not our own.

Genesis 16:1–12,15–16 or 16:6b–12,15–16
Psalm 106:1b–2,3–4a,4b–5
Matthew 7:21–29

[Jesus said,] "There will be more joy in heaven
over one sinner who repents
than over ninety-nine righteous people
who have no need of repentance."
—LUKE 15:7

Jesus came looking for the lost sheep. He still seeks those
who are wandering, hurt, alone, frightened, and confused.
Dear Lord, develop in your people the deep compassion you
have for those who are lost from you.

Ezekiel 34:11–16
Psalm 23:1–3a,3b–4,5,6 (1)
Romans 5:5b–11
Luke 15:3–7

• THE IMMACULATE HEART OF THE BLESSED VIRGIN MARY •

"He has filled the hungry with good things,
and the rich he has sent away empty."
—LUKE 1:53

So many sayings in Scripture are paradoxical: The last will be first; to be the greatest, you must become a servant, and so on. And here, the Lord counteracts the natural order of things, giving priority to the hungry and ignoring those with power and wealth. If it is possible, Lord Jesus, teach us to see life as you do.

Genesis 18:1–15
Luke 1:46–47,48–49,50 and 53,54–55
Matthew 8:5–17
Or, for the Optional Memorial of the Immaculate Heart, Genesis 18:1–15 / Luke 2:41–51

Sunday

JUNE 29

I want you to know, brothers and sisters,
that the Gospel preached by me is not of human origin.
For I did not receive it from a human being, nor was I taught it,
but it came through a revelation of Jesus Christ.
—GALATIANS 1:11–12

Ultimately, every one of us must receive the truth from Jesus himself. In that encounter with the Christ, the very soul is convinced and will never forget the truth of the experience.

VIGIL:	DAY:
Acts 3:1–10	Acts 12:1–11
Psalm 19:2–3,4–5	Psalm 34:2–3,4–5,6–7,8–9
Galatians 1:11–20	2 Timothy 4:6–8,17–18
John 21:15–19	Matthew 16:13–19

Merciful and gracious is the LORD,
slow to anger and abounding in kindness.
—PSALM 103:8

Abraham knew that God is merciful and gracious; in the
Genesis reading for today, Abraham bargains with God. He
begins by asking if God will spare Sodom if there are fifty
righteous people in it, and God says he will spare it. Then,
reconsidering, Abraham offers lower numbers, finally ending
with ten. God agrees to spare the city for the sake of only
ten righteous people. By this point in his life, Abraham
understands that he can speak honestly with God, ask
questions of God, even make requests. This is an early
picture of friendship between God and humanity.

Genesis 18:16–33
Psalm 103:1b–2,3–4,8–9,10–11
Matthew 8:18–22

Tuesday

JULY 1

• ST. JUNIPERO SERRA, PRIEST •

Search me, O LORD, and try me;
test my soul and my heart.
For your mercy is before my eyes,
and I walk in your truth.
—PSALM 26:2–3

If anyone must search and try me, I greatly prefer a judge who is merciful and honest. God searches me not to torment me but to help me—to turn away from what is harmful, to learn the best way to live, to be truthful with myself. Yes, of course, search, try, and test me. Help me grow.

Genesis 19:15–29
Psalm 26:2–3,9–10,11–12
Matthew 8:23–27

⇒ 213 ⇐

Wednesday
JULY 2

The demons pleaded with him,
"If you drive us out, send us into the herd of swine."
And he said to them, "Go then!"
—MATTHEW 8:31–32

This is not such a little detail, that Jesus spoke with the
demons; they made a request, and he granted it. I don't really
know what to make of it. The demons recognized Jesus and
his power over them. In no such encounter of the Gospels do
they challenge his authority; rather, they plead with him.
Perhaps we would not be so fearful if we remembered that
the Jesus to whose Body we belong has such authority that
we need not fear even the demons.

Genesis 21:5,8–20a
Psalm 34:7–8,10–11,12–13
Matthew 8:28–34

Thursday

JULY 3

• ST. THOMAS, APOSTLE •

But Thomas said to them,
"Unless I see the mark of the nails in his hands
and put my finger into the nailmarks
and put my hand into his side, I will not believe."
—JOHN 20:25

I'm giving Thomas the benefit of the doubt here. In these chaotic days of Jesus' trial and crucifixion, Thomas was taking no chances, unwilling to believe just anybody who showed up saying they were the risen Jesus. Maybe Thomas doubted the Resurrection itself, but it's possible that he suspected an imposter was sent to lure Jesus' followers to the Romans. Whatever the case, Thomas is honest at least. As we all should be, whether in doubt or in faith.

Ephesians 2:19–22
Psalm 117:1bc,2
John 20:24–29

Friday

JULY 4

• INDEPENDENCE DAY •

*The Pharisees saw this and said to his disciples,
"Why does your teacher eat with tax collectors and sinners?"*
—MATTHEW 9:11

You can know something about a person by the questions he
asks. Is he seeking to understand something? Is he looking
for a weakness? Is he trying to intimidate? Does he want to
know the person better? From the Pharisees' words alone, it's
hard to tell their motivation. Were they in fact curious about
Jesus' methodology or his theology? But notice their focus:
sinners. They even used the term *sinners*, not *people*. Their
curiosity centered on who was in and who was out. What do
your questions say about you?

Genesis 23:1–4,19; 24:1–8,62–67
Psalm 106:1b–2,3–4a,4b–5
Matthew 9:9–13
Or, for Independence Day, any readings from the Mass "For the Country or a City"
(882–886), or the Mass "For Peace and Justice" (887–891)

⇒ 216 ⇐

Saturday

JULY 5

Rebekah had been listening while Isaac was speaking to his son Esau.
So, when Esau went out into the country
to hunt some game for his father,
Rebekah [then] took the best clothes of her older son Esau
that she had in the house,
and gave them to her younger son Jacob to wear.
—GENESIS 27:5,15

Ah, the scheming mother. It's no wonder Jacob turned out to be such a trickster. We wonder how many other times during her sons' lives Rebekah had favored Jacob over Esau and manipulated circumstances in Jacob's favor. To be fair, Isaac favored Esau, so neither parent was impartial. Not the best environment for bringing up children.

Genesis 27:1–5,15–29
Psalm 135:1b–2,3–4,5–6
Matthew 9:14–17

Sunday

JULY 6

May I never boast except in the cross of our Lord Jesus Christ,
through which the world has been crucified to me,
and I to the world.
For neither does circumcision mean anything, nor does uncircumcision
but only a new creation.
—GALATIANS 6:14–15

The apostle Paul was a thoroughly trained scholar in
Judaism. It's no small thing for him to dismiss circumcision, a
ritual and mark that set apart the Jewish people from other
nations. Such identifiers no longer matter. Everything is
defined by Christ and our relationship to him. We can aim to
be indifferent about any other brand or status symbol.

Isaiah 66:10–14c
Psalm 66:1–3,4–5,6–7,16,20 (1)
Galatians 6:14–18
Luke 10:1–12,17–20 or 10:1–9

Monday
JULY 7

When Jacob awoke from his sleep, he exclaimed,
"Truly, the LORD is in this spot, although I did not know it!"
In solemn wonder he cried out: "How awesome is this shrine!
This is nothing else but an abode of God,
and that is the gateway to heaven!"
—GENESIS 28:16–17

Here's a good prayer exercise. Reflect on your history and identify a time when you realized "Truly, the LORD is in this spot, although I did not know it!" So often we recognize grace in retrospect. Allow the Holy Spirit to guide you to some holy memories.

Genesis 28:10–22a
Psalm 91:1–2,3–4,14–15ab
Matthew 9:18–26

Hide me in the shadow of your wings.
I in justice shall behold your face;
on waking, I shall be content in your presence.
—PSALM 17:8B AND 15

The psalmist uses the comforting image of a mother hen's
wings that shelter the chicks. It's such a safe place that a
person wakes up in contentment. What adds to this peaceful
scene is justice. Indeed, justice leads to peace, which makes
for safety. May we remember justice while working for peace.

Genesis 32:23–33
Psalm 17:1b,2–3,6–7ab,8b and 15
Matthew 9:32–38

Wednesday

JULY 9

• ST. AUGUSTINE ZHAO RONG, PRIEST, AND COMPANIONS, MARTYRS •

Jesus sent out these Twelve after instructing them thus,
"Do not go into pagan territory or enter a Samaritan town.
Go rather to the lost sheep of the house of Israel."
—MATTHEW 10:5–6

Jesus was a Jew, sent to his own people to announce the
coming of God's kingdom. We know that the Good News
was meant, ultimately, for the whole world, including each of
us. But it had to start somewhere. Jesus started in his own
environment, among his own people. Every powerful
movement begins at home.

Genesis 41:55–57; 42:5–7a,17–24a
Psalm 33:2–3,10–11,18–19
Matthew 10:1–7

Thursday

JULY 10

[Jesus said,]
"Whatever town or village you enter, look for a worthy person in it,
and stay there until you leave.
As you enter a house, wish it peace."
—MATTHEW 10:11–12

Throughout life, it's wise to look for "worthy" people—those
who share our values, those we can trust to be honest,
faithful, compassionate. When we have just a few worthy
people to accompany us, we can navigate
ever-changing situations.

Genesis 44:18–21,23b–29; 45:1–5
Psalm 105:16–17,18–19,20–21
Matthew 10:7–15

Jesus said to his disciples,
"Behold, I am sending you like sheep in the midst of wolves;
so be shrewd as serpents and simple as doves."
—MATTHEW 10:16

Jesus instructs his apostles to be shrewd, so we might consider what it means to be shrewd today. *Shrewd* probably includes being well-informed, able to think critically, open to conversation and negotiation, and good at sorting out the truth. A shrewd person is smart—but also wise.

Genesis 46:1–7,28–30
Psalm 37:3–4,18–19,27–28,39–40
Matthew 10:16–23

Saturday

JULY 12

Jesus said to his disciples,
"No disciple is above his teacher,
no slave above his master.
It is enough for the disciple that he become like his teacher,
for the slave that he become like his master."
—MATTHEW 10:24–25

May we remember Jesus' words when life gets hard, when people misunderstand us, when we're asked to serve others, when our way of life feels like swimming against the stream.

Genesis 49:29–32; 50:15–26a
Psalm 105:1–2,3–4,6–7
Matthew 10:24–33

Sunday

JULY 13

• FIFTEENTH SUNDAY IN ORDINARY TIME •

For this command that I enjoin on you today
is not too mysterious and remote for you. . . .
No, it is something very near to you,
already in your mouths and in your hearts;
you have only to carry it out.
—DEUTERONOMY 30:11,14

So many times, when we're looking for direction or an
answer, we expect new information. When, all along, God
was preparing us, was teaching us what we need for the
moment we now face. The Holy Spirit dwells within us; we
already contain much more wisdom and knowledge
than we recognize.

Deuteronomy 30:10–14
Psalm 69:14,17,30–31,33–34,36,37
Colossians 1:15–20
Luke 10:25–37

Monday

JULY 14

• ST. KATERI TEKAKWITHA, VIRGIN •

*The Egyptians, then, dreaded the children of Israel
and reduced them to cruel slavery,
making life bitter for them with hard work in mortar and brick
and all kinds of field work—the whole cruel fate of slaves.*

—EXODUS 1:12–13

When there got to be too many Israelites in Egypt, the
Egyptians worried that these outsiders—immigrants—would
acquire too much wealth and power. The solution: enslave
them, break them down with hard labor, dehumanize them.
Fear of immigrants is still with us, isn't it? Not just in the
United States but pretty much everywhere in the world. It's
when we fear people that we're most likely to mistreat them.

Exodus 1:8–14,22
Psalm 124:1b–3,4–6,7–8
Matthew 10:34—11:1

⇉ 226 ⇇

Tuesday

JULY 15

Jesus began to reproach the towns
where most of his mighty deeds had been done,
since they had not repented.
"Woe to you, Chorazin! Woe to you, Bethsaida!
For if the mighty deeds done in your midst
had been done in Tyre and Sidon,
they would long ago have repented in sackcloth and ashes."
—MATTHEW 11:20–21

Do I witness great wonders, mighty works, in my own life, yet dismiss them? Have I become so accustomed to being loved and forgiven that I devalue those graces? Do transformative acts of others' charity go by me, undetected? Jesus says to us today, "Pay attention! The kingdom of God is at hand."

Exodus 2:1–15a
Psalm 69:3,14,30–31,33–34
Matthew 11:20–24

Wednesday

JULY 16

• OUR LADY OF MOUNT CARMEL •

At that time Jesus exclaimed:
"I give praise to you, Father, Lord of heaven and earth,
for although you have hidden these things
from the wise and the learned
you have revealed them to the childlike."
—MATTHEW 11:25

Sometimes the wisest person in the room is not the one with the most education, wealth, or influence. Sometimes a young person will make an observation that we need to acknowledge and learn from. Sometimes an elderly aunt or grandpa can offer better advice than a Google search. God looks for an open heart, and no matter whose heart that is, the Holy Spirit blesses it with wisdom. Be on the lookout!

Exodus 3:1–6,9–12
Psalm 103:1b–2,3–4,6–7
Matthew 11:25–27

Thursday

JULY 17

*Yet I know that the king of Egypt will not allow you to go
unless he is forced.
I will stretch out my hand, therefore,
and smite Egypt by doing all kinds of wondrous deeds there.
After that he will send you away.*
—EXODUS 3:19–20

Our God is not coercive when it comes to transforming our hearts. We are invited into relationship with divine love, not manipulated into it. But God works powerfully to liberate us, just as God performed mighty and frightening works to free the Israelites. Thank you, Lord, for your great power, used in love.

Exodus 3:13–20
Psalm 105:1 and 5,8–9,24–25,26–27
Matthew 11:28–30

Friday

JULY 18

• ST. CAMILLUS DE LELLIS, PRIEST •

*How shall I make a return to the LORD
for all the good he has done for me?
The cup of salvation I will take up,
and I will call upon the name of the LORD.*
—PSALM 116:12–13

What does God ask of us? Simple gratitude. A relationship intimate enough that we turn to God for what we need, that we call on God for help. Simply turn to the Lord—that's adequate "payment" for all our blessings.

Exodus 11:10—12:14
Psalm 116:12–13,15 and 16bc,17–18
Matthew 12:1–8

Saturday

JULY 19

The children of Israel set out from Rameses for Succoth,
about six hundred thousand men on foot,
not counting the little ones.
A crowd of mixed ancestry also went up with them,
besides their livestock, very numerous flocks and herds.
—EXODUS 12:37–38

When we read the history of Israel, we tend to forget about the "crowd of mixed ancestry" who also left Egypt with them. We can safely assume that, throughout Israel's history, people of other nations and races were included in their community. Even from the beginning, God's care and salvation reached beyond one group of people. It was never so much about bloodline as it was about a developing relationship of trust between people and the God who loved them.

Exodus 12:37–42
Psalm 136:1 and 23–24,10–12,13–15
Matthew 12:14–21

Sunday

JULY 20

• SIXTEENTH SUNDAY IN ORDINARY TIME •

Now I rejoice in my sufferings for your sake,
and in my flesh I am filling up
what is lacking in the afflictions of Christ
on behalf of his body, which is the church.
—COLOSSIANS 1:24

My suffering is more than just my suffering. Because I am part of the Body of Christ, my suffering is joined with Christ's suffering. My suffering is intertwined with the suffering of others. We're in this together—the suffering as well as the healing. I pray that, whenever I suffer, the experience will draw me closer to God and to other people.

Genesis 18:1–10a
Psalm 15:2–3,3–4,5 (1a)
Colossians 1:24–28
Luke 10:38–42

⇒ 232 ⇐

"Why did you bring us out of Egypt?
Did we not tell you this in Egypt, when we said,
'Leave us alone. Let us serve the Egyptians'?"
—EXODUS 14:11–12

Is it possible to prefer a harder life because it's familiar?
Might we rather serve false gods because they are easier to
comprehend? After generations of hard slavery, the Israelites
would rather go back to Egypt and become slaves again than
follow God into the unknown future. It's not difficult to
empathize with them. We like to know what's coming. We
like to feel as if we have some control over our situation. This
can lead us to back away from our adventure called faith.

Exodus 14:5–18
Exodus 15:1bc–2,3–4,5–6
Matthew 12:38–42

⟩ 233 ⟨

Tuesday

JULY 22

• ST. MARY MAGDALENE •

The Bride says,
On my bed at night I sought him
whom my heart loves—
I sought him but I did not find him. . . .
I will rise then and go about the city;
in the streets and crossings I will seek
him whom my heart loves.
—SONG OF SONGS 3:1–2

The intensity and tenacity of the desire described in this love
poem has, through the ages, inspired people in their search
for connection with God. Our most intimate love offers a
glimpse, a glimmer of love between God and humanity.
When we enjoy the sexual union of marriage, we experience
a taste of higher, deeper, eternal love.

Song of Songs 3:1–4b or 2 Corinthians 5:14–17
Exodus 15:8–9,10 and 12,17
John 20:1–2,11–18

≥ 234 ≤

Wednesday

JULY 23

• ST. BRIDGET OF SWEDEN, RELIGIOUS •

On seeing it, the children of Israel asked one another, "What is this?"
for they did not know what it was.
But Moses told them,
"This is the bread which the LORD has given you to eat."
—EXODUS 16:15

Sometimes I need an interpreter. God offers me a gift, and I don't truly see it. I don't recognize or understand it. So God sends someone—a teacher, an elder, a friend, or spiritual director—to open my eyes to this new reality. This is why the Christian life is not a lone endeavor; we need one another. We can help each other see what God is doing right in front of us.

Exodus 16:1–5,9–15
Psalm 78:18–19,23–24,25–26,27–28
Matthew 13:1–9

⇒ 235 ⇐

Thursday

JULY 24

• ST. SHARBEL MAKHLŪF, PRIEST •

On the morning of the third day
there were peals of thunder and lightning,
and a heavy cloud over the mountain,
and a very loud trumpet blast,
so that all the people in the camp trembled.
But Moses led the people out of the camp to meet God,
and they stationed themselves at the foot of the mountain.
—EXODUS 19:16–17

A person might be afraid of God, for various reasons, such as hurtful experiences connected with church or abusive treatment from a parent or other authority figure. At such times, a person could use a companion, someone to, so to speak, make introductions. Just think: you might be that companion for someone.

Exodus 19:1–2,9–11,16–20b
Daniel 3:52,53,54,55,56
Matthew 13:10–17

Friday

JULY 25

• ST. JAMES, APOSTLE •

We are afflicted in every way, but not constrained;
perplexed, but not driven to despair;
persecuted, but not abandoned;
struck down, but not destroyed;
always carrying about in the body the dying of Jesus,
so that the life of Jesus may be manifested in our body.
For we who live are constantly being given up to death
for the sake of Jesus,
so that the life of Jesus may be manifested in our mortal flesh.
—2 CORINTHIANS 4:8–11

The writer offers a powerful statement, one that can temper
our expectations. While we cannot hope to escape the
normal trials of life, certainly we can reframe our view. We
carry in our bodies the Paschal mystery of Christ crucified,
buried, and risen. We ourselves now contain the entire
mystery of life and death. It is a trial at times, yes, but
also a privilege.

2 Corinthians 4:7–15
Psalm 126:1bc–2ab,2cd–3,4–5,6
Matthew 20:20–28

Saturday

JULY 26

• ST. JOACHIM AND ST. ANNE, PARENTS OF THE BLESSED VIRGIN MARY •

Jesus proposed a parable to the crowds.
"The Kingdom of heaven may be likened to a man
who sowed good seed in his field.
While everyone was asleep his enemy came
and sowed weeds all through the wheat, and then went off.
When the crop grew and bore fruit, the weeds appeared as well."
—MATTHEW 13:24–26

In any good work, there are bound to be "weeds among the wheat." No reason to be surprised when difficulties spring up as we go through the day, minding our own business. No reason to feel that God is trying to teach us something or that we somehow brought this on ourselves. The weeds will pop up. But we will keep growing.

Exodus 24:3–8
Psalm 50:1b–2,5–6,14–15
Matthew 13:24–30

And even when you were dead
in transgressions and the uncircumcision of your flesh,
he brought you to life along with him,
having forgiven us all our transgressions;
obliterating the bond against us, with its legal claims,
which was opposed to us,
he also removed it from our midst, nailing it to the cross.
—COLOSSIANS 2:13–14

Do I begin to comprehend what these verses mean? We have
been brought to life along with Jesus. Our wrongs, sins,
weaknesses, failures, have been nailed to the cross. We are
already alive. Already helped. Already forgiven.

Genesis 18:20–32
Psalm 138:1–2,2–3,6–7,7–8 (3a)
Colossians 2:12–14
Luke 11:1–13

[Jesus] spoke to them another parable.
"The Kingdom of heaven is like yeast
that a woman took and mixed with three measures of wheat flour
until the whole batch was leavened."
—MATTHEW 13:33

Hope spreads. So do compassion, wisdom, peace, and truth.
These graces spread so quietly, so steadily, that we hardly
notice it at the time. Know that whatever virtue you practice
will have an impact: here or there, now or later.

Exodus 32:15–24,30–34
Psalm 106:19–20,21–22,23
Matthew 13:31–35

Tuesday

JULY 29

• ST. MARTHA, ST. MARY, AND ST. LAZARUS •

When Martha heard that Jesus was coming,
she went to meet him;
but Mary sat at home.
—JOHN 11:20

Of the sisters Mary and Martha, Martha has often been cast
as the one with less faith, less devotion to Jesus. But John's
account is pretty stark: Martha went to meet Jesus, but Mary
did not. Their brother had just died—because Jesus delayed
in coming to help him. I imagine Mary sitting in the house,
refusing to meet the friend who has disappointed her hopes
for her brother's healing. Martha, ever the one showing
hospitality, hurries to meet Jesus and talk with him about
what has happened. Faith works through each
unique personality.

Exodus 33:7–11; 34:5b–9,28
Psalm 103:6–7,8–9,10–11,12–13
John 11:19–27 or Luke 10:38–42

When Aaron, then, and the other children of Israel saw Moses
and noticed how radiant the skin of his face had become,
they were afraid to come near him. . . .
Later on, all the children of Israel came up to him,
and he enjoined on them all that the LORD
had told him on Mount Sinai.
—EXODUS 34:30–32

We see another instance when the people are afraid to come close to holiness. They don't know what might happen. They don't understand that a powerful God can also be gentle. Moses becomes the buffer zone, and the people come closer to God by approaching Moses. Lord God, may I become a buffer zone to those who are afraid of you or who do not understand your love.

Exodus 34:29–35
Psalm 99:5,6,7,9
Matthew 13:44–46

Thursday

JULY 31

[Jesus] replied,
"Then every scribe who has been instructed in the Kingdom of heaven
is like the head of a household who brings from his storeroom
both the new and the old."
—MATTHEW 13:52

There's a place for education and history in the life of faith.
We turn to our scholars, who can unlock information they
worked years to decipher. We turn to our teachers, whose
job it is to understand how belief can influence life. We turn
to our elders, who remember good times and bad times, can
remind us of past mistakes and accomplishments. Today, say
a prayer of thanks for the people who
have been "scribes" for you.

Exodus 40:16–21,34–38
Psalm 84:3,4,5–6a and 8a,11
Matthew 13:47–53

Jesus came to his native place and taught the people in their synagogue.
They were astonished and said,
"Where did this man get such wisdom and mighty deeds?
Is he not the carpenter's son?"
—MATTHEW 13:54–55

It's difficult for people to adjust their thinking about a person.
When we're growing up, everyone around us gets to know
us, and, very early, they form their opinions about us. People
in Jesus' hometown could see him only as the carpenter's son,
and they resisted seeing Jesus as the man God had called him
to be. When we follow our own calling, we can take courage
from Jesus' example and not be held back by the
views of others.

Leviticus 23:1,4–11,15–16,27,34b–37
Psalm 81:3–4,5–6,10–11ab
Matthew 13:54–58

Saturday

AUGUST 2

• ST. EUSEBIUS OF VERCELLI, BISHOP • ST. PETER JULIAN EYMARD, PRIEST •

This fiftieth year you shall make sacred
by proclaiming liberty in the land for all its inhabitants.
—LEVITICUS 25:10

God gave the Israelites guidelines for living justly and
mercifully. Every fifty years, debts were to be forgiven and
other measures were taken so that all the people had the
opportunity to start over. These practices, if followed, would
prevent a few people from having excess while others
languished in poverty. We don't know if these sacred Jubilee
guidelines were followed consistently, but certainly we can
be guided by them in some fashion today, making room for
people to recover from losses and start fresh.

Leviticus 25:1,8–17
Psalm 67:2–3,5,7–8
Matthew 14:1–12

⇒ 245 ⇐

Sunday

AUGUST 3

• EIGHTEENTH SUNDAY IN ORDINARY TIME •

For what profit comes to a man from all the toil and anxiety of heart
with which he has labored under the sun?
All his days sorrow and grief are their occupation;
even at night his mind is not at rest.
This also is vanity.
—ECCLESIASTES 1:2; 2:23

In the United States, we have come to idolize overwork. We
admire people who labor excessive hours, who have so many
projects and responsibilities that they are always busy, always
tired, yet carry the pride of accomplishment. The wisdom
writer who gave us the sayings in Ecclesiastes has a different
view. It's quite foolish to work long hours and be constantly
occupied. Which view will influence the way I live?

Ecclesiastes 1:2; 2:21–23
Psalm 90:3–4,5–6,12–13,14,17 (1)
Colossians 3:1–5,9–11
Luke 12:13–21

⇒ 246 ⇐

[Moses said to the Lord,]
"I cannot carry all this people by myself,
for they are too heavy for me.
If this is the way you will deal with me,
then please do me the favor of killing me at once,
so that I need no longer face this distress."
—NUMBERS 11:14–15

It's nice to know that even a great leader of Israel had his bad
days and drama-queen moments. Moses is saying, "Just kill
me now." He was overwhelmed by his leadership
responsibilities. Just as a mother is overwhelmed some days
by her parenting role or any one of us feels that we can't go
on carrying the load we've been given. Rather than simmer in
resentment and self-pity, Moses took his complaint to God,
which is what we can do, even on our worst days.

Numbers 11:4b–15
Psalm 81:12–13,14–15,16–17
Matthew 14:22–36 or 14:13–21

AUGUST 5

• THE DEDICATION OF THE BASILICA OF ST. MARY MAJOR •

Jesus made the disciples get into a boat
and precede him to the other side of the sea,
while he dismissed the crowds.
After doing so, he went up on the mountain by himself to pray.
—MATTHEW 14:22–24

I love this scene! Jesus sends away the disciples and dismisses
the crowds. When he finally gets rid of everybody, he goes
away to pray. We know that he loved his disciples and was
compassionate toward the needy crowds, but he was wise
enough to recognize when it was time to refuel on his own. If
Jesus needed his alone time, then certainly I do too.

Numbers 12:1–13
Psalm 51:3–4,5–6ab,6cd–7,12–13
Matthew 14:22–36 or 15:1–2,10–14

AUGUST 6

• THE TRANSFIGURATION OF THE LORD •

As I watched in the night visions,
I saw one like a Son of man coming,
One like a Son of man coming,
on the clouds of heaven;
when he reached the Ancient One
and was presented before him,
the one like a Son of man received dominion, glory, and kingship;
all the peoples, nations, and languages serve him.
His dominion is an everlasting dominion
that shall not be taken away,
his kingship shall not be destroyed.
—DANIEL 7:13–14

This is a scene to linger with, to savor. We know Jesus as friend and savior, but pause with these verses from Daniel and ponder Jesus as the One over all. His dominion is everlasting—and we are part of that.

Daniel 7:9–10,13–14
Psalm 97:1–2,5–6,9
2 Peter 1:16–19
Luke 9:28b–36

AUGUST 7

• ST. SIXTUS II, POPE, AND COMPANIONS, MARTYRS * ST. CAJETAN, PRIEST •

Jesus went into the region of Caesarea Philippi
and he asked his disciples,
"Who do people say that the Son of Man is?"
They replied, "Some say John the Baptist, others Elijah,
still others Jeremiah or one of the prophets."
He said to them, "But who do you say that I am?"
—MATTHEW 16:13–15

Caesarea Philippi was the most pagan area of Palestine. It was the location of multiple temples to multiple gods. This is where Jesus took his disciples—they certainly would have avoided the place otherwise—and asked them, "Who do you say that I am?" He was pressing them to see him in the context of all other gods. As we are ready, Jesus reveals himself to us in greater fullness.

Numbers 20:1–13
Psalm 95:1–2,6–7,8–9
Matthew 16:13–23

AUGUST 8

• ST. DOMINIC, PRIEST •

[Moses said,]
"Did a people ever hear the voice of God
speaking from the midst of fire, as you did, and live?
Or did any god venture to go and take a nation for himself
from the midst of another nation,
by testings, by signs and wonders, by war . . .
all of which the LORD, your God,
did for you in Egypt before your very eyes?"
—DEUTERONOMY 4:33–34

Moses reminds the people of how privileged they are to be
the focus of God's care and provision. How might you
rewrite Moses' words to remind yourself today of God's care
for you?

Deuteronomy 4:32–40
Psalm 77:12–13,14–15,16 and 21
Matthew 16:24–28

"When, therefore, you eat your fill,
take care not to forget the LORD,
who brought you out of the land of Egypt, that place of slavery."
—DEUTERONOMY 6:11–12

The Lord knew that when things are going well, we tend to
forget whose strength and providence we rely on. May we
take care to remember God when we have plenty, when
there are no pressing problems. During the good times, we
can practice gratitude.

Deuteronomy 6:4–13
Psalm 18:2–3a,3bc–4,47 and 51
Matthew 17:14–20

[Jesus said to his disciples,]
"Do not be afraid any longer, little flock,
for your Father is pleased to give you the kingdom."
—LUKE 12:32

Notice how gentle Jesus' language is here. He calls the people "little flock" and stresses that the Father is "pleased" to give them the kingdom. Can you hear God's love for you in Jesus' words? Can you believe, truly believe, that God is pleased, happy, to give you what you need?

Wisdom 18:6–9
Psalm 33:1,12,18–19,20–22 (12b)
Hebrews 11:1–2,8–19 or 11:1–2,8–12
Luke 12:32–48 or 12:35–40

AUGUST 11

• ST. CLARE, VIRGIN •

As Jesus and his disciples were gathering in Galilee,
Jesus said to them,
"The Son of Man is to be handed over to men,
and they will kill him, and he will be raised on the third day."
And they were overwhelmed with grief.
—MATTHEW 17:22–23

It wasn't always pleasant to be a disciple of Jesus, especially toward the end, when he spoke of what would happen to him. The disciples were with their beloved leader and teacher, yet they grieved. Even in his presence they were overwhelmed. Perhaps we should remember this on days when, despite believing in the Lord's constant presence, we are overcome with sadness, grief, inner disturbance. God designed us to be emotional, and God knows the limits of our understanding.

Deuteronomy 10:12–22
Psalm 147:12–13,14–15,19–20
Matthew 17:22–27

[Jesus said to his disciples,]
"If a man has a hundred sheep and one of them goes astray,
will he not leave the ninety-nine in the hills
and go in search of the stray?"
—MATTHEW 18:12

Popular culture conditions us to side with the strongest person, to identify with the winners, to be drawn to people who are successful and influential. Jesus expresses to his disciples the divine view of life: God focuses on the lost, the weak, the left-out.

Deuteronomy 31:1–8
Deuteronomy 32:3–4ab,7,8,9 and 12
Matthew 18:1–5,10,12–14

Since then no prophet has arisen in Israel like Moses,
whom the LORD knew face to face.
—DEUTERONOMY 34:10

Lord God, help me become the kind of person who knows you face-to-face. It seems impossible that I could become a friend of God of the Universe, but that's what I want to be.

Deuteronomy 34:1–12
Psalm 66:1–3a,5 and 8,16–17
Matthew 18:15–20

Thursday

AUGUST 14

• ST. MAXIMILIAN MARY KOLBE, PRIEST AND MARTYR •

Peter approached Jesus and asked him,
"Lord, if my brother sins against me,
how often must I forgive him?
As many as seven times?"
—MATTHEW 18:21

Was Peter looking for a forgiveness loophole? Was he hoping Jesus would give him a number, and after that Peter would not have to forgive the person who kept offending him? Or did Peter think that perhaps God put a limit on forgiveness, that there was a rule somewhere to tell us when we've gone too far? What do I prefer—a magic number or limitless mercy?

Joshua 3:7–10a,11,13–17
Psalm 114:1–2,3–4,5–6
Matthew 18:21—19:1

AUGUST 15

• THE ASSUMPTION OF THE BLESSED VIRGIN MARY •

Then the dragon stood before the woman about to give birth,
to devour her child when she gave birth.
She gave birth to a son, a male child,
destined to rule all the nations with an iron rod.
Her child was caught up to God and his throne.
The woman herself fled into the desert
where she had a place prepared by God.
—REVELATION 12:4–6

This vision of John reveals the birth of Jesus, whom Satan
plans to devour. But the child is caught up to God, and the
mother is kept safe. May we keep in mind that, beyond all
the schemes of evil in this world, there is the ultimate reality
of saving grace.

VIGIL:	DAY:
1 Chronicles 15:3–4,15–16; 16:1–2	Revelation 11:19a; 12:1–6a,10ab
Psalm 132:6–7,9–10,13–14	Psalm 45:10,11,12,16
1 Corinthians 15:54b–57	1 Corinthians 15:20–27
Luke 11:27–28	Luke 1:39–56

AUGUST 16

• ST. STEPHEN OF HUNGARY •

Joshua therefore said to the people,
"You are your own witnesses that you have chosen to serve the LORD."
They replied, "We are, indeed!"
Joshua continued,
"Now, therefore, put away the strange gods that are among you
and turn your hearts to the LORD, the God of Israel."
—JOSHUA 24:22,23

I chose God early; I invited Jesus into my life when I was still a child. Since those days, I have chosen Jesus again and again. And I have had to reject other gods—money, reputation, power, self-interest—numerous times. In fact, every time I partake of Christ's body and blood, I make this crucial choice once again.

Joshua 24:14–29
Psalm 16:1–2a and 5,7–8,11
Matthew 19:13–15

Sunday

AUGUST 17

• TWENTIETH SUNDAY IN ORDINARY TIME •

Jesus said to his disciples,
"I have come to set the earth on fire,
and how I wish it were already blazing!
There is a baptism with which I must be baptized,
and how great is my anguish until it is accomplished!"
—LUKE 12:49–50

These verses remind me of the term *creative destruction*. For a new thing to be created, the current situation must be dismantled, even destroyed. Jesus knew that people could not experience the kingdom of God without also experiencing the destruction of their own broken world. Can we welcome Christ's renewal in us, knowing that it will require the loss of life as it now is?

Jeremiah 38:4–6,8–10
Psalm 40:2,3,4,18 (14b)
Hebrews 12:1–4
Luke 12:49–53

Monday

AUGUST 18

*Whatever they undertook, the LORD turned into disaster for them,
as in his warning he had sworn he would do,
till they were in great distress.*
—JUDGES 2:15

In God's great love for us, God usually does not "bless" us
when we are living in a way that is harmful or
counterproductive. Why would God give positive
reinforcement for ways that are not life-giving? Rather, God
allows a bad situation to play itself out. God allows us to be
in distress. The hope is that, eventually, we will change
direction and correct our ways, for our good.

Judges 2:11–19
Psalm 106:34–35,36–37,39–40,43ab and 44
Matthew 19:16–22

The angel of the LORD appeared to [Gideon] and said,
"The LORD is with you, O champion!"
Gideon said to him, "My Lord, if the LORD is with us,
why has all this happened to us?"
—JUDGES 6:12–13

Isn't this wonderful storytelling? Can you imagine an ordinary guy replying to a heavenly messenger, "Um, given the wreck our lives have become, I sort of doubt the God-is-with-you part." I've noticed, though, that God rarely, if ever, scolds anyone for being honest. God loves our questions. God wants us to engage in real conversation.

Judges 6:11–24a
Psalm 85:9,11–12,13–14
Matthew 19:23–30

AUGUST 20

• ST. BERNARD OF CLAIRVAUX, ABBOT AND DOCTOR OF THE CHURCH •

[The landowner said,]
"My friend, I am not cheating you.
Did you not agree with me for the usual daily wage?
Take what is yours and go.
What if I wish to give this last one the same as you?
Or am I not free to do as I wish with my own money?
Are you envious because I am generous?"
—MATTHEW 20:13–15

We sinful human beings tend to have an overactive concept
of justice. We are rankled at the thought of someone getting
what they don't deserve. This often leads to blaming the
victim. We believe that a person is poor because that's what
he or she deserves. Certainly, that person should not receive
charity! This parable should cure us of that attitude. Why
should we be envious of God's generosity?

Judges 9:6–15
Psalm 21:2–3,4–5,6–7
Matthew 20:1–16

Thursday

AUGUST 21

• ST. PIUS X, POPE •

Sacrifice or oblation you wished not,
but ears open to obedience you gave me.
Burnt offerings or sin-offerings you sought not,
then said I, "Behold I come."
—PSALM 40:7–8

God wants my cooperation, that's all. That cooperation may
lead to offerings, service, even personal sacrifice. But none of
that matters if I withhold myself.

Judges 11:29–39a
Psalm 40:5,7–8a,8b–9,10
Matthew 22:1–14

⇒264⇐

• THE QUEENSHIP OF THE BLESSED VIRGIN MARY •

[Jesus] said to him,
"You shall love the Lord, your God, with all your heart,
with all your soul, and with all your mind.
This is the greatest and the first commandment.
The second is like it:
You shall love your neighbor as yourself.
The whole law and the prophets depend on these two commandments."
—MATTHEW 22:37–40

What if, in every situation, we asked these questions: *What would love look like right now? What would love do?* Are you willing to carry out this experiment for the next day or two?

Ruth 1:1,3–6,14b–16,22
Psalm 146:5–6ab,6c–7,8–9a,9bc–10
Matthew 22:34–40

Saturday

AUGUST 23

• ST. ROSE OF LIMA, VIRGIN •

Boaz answered [Ruth,]
"I have had a complete account of what you have done
for your mother-in-law after your husband's death;
you have left your father and your mother and the land of your birth,
and have come to a people whom you did not know previously."
—RUTH 2:11

People notice what kind of person you are. They may not say
anything to you, but your manner, your words, and your
actions make an impression. Learn to trust this. Go about
your life intentionally, discerning what is best, doing what
seems right, treating others kindly. The rest will work
itself out.

Ruth 2:1–3,8–11; 4:13–17
Psalm 128:1b–2,3,4,5
Matthew 23:1–12

AUGUST 24

• TWENTY-FIRST SUNDAY IN ORDINARY TIME •

At the time,
all discipline seems a cause not for joy but for pain,
yet later it brings the peaceful fruit of righteousness
to those who are trained by it.
—HEBREWS 12:11

An employee disciplines herself not to react when the
supervisor is blunt or impetuous. The parent disciplines
himself to apologize to the teenager after an argument goes
out of control. One person trains himself not to obsess over
his physical appearance, and another learns by practice to
pause before assuming that she must solve everybody's
problems. We are always in training. But the results are
worth it.

Isaiah 66:18–21
Psalm 117:1,2
Hebrews 12:5–7,11–13
Luke 13:22–30

For our Gospel did not come to you in word alone,
but also in power and in the Holy Spirit and with much conviction.
—1 THESSALONIANS 1:5

It's easy to become so involved in our message to people that
we forget how much we depend on the Holy Spirit to help
that message hit home. If we inundate people with words,
after a while they grow immune to what we're trying to say.
But if we choose our words wisely and work in concert with
the Holy Spirit, the words will find people when they are
ready for the message.

1 Thessalonians 1:1–5,8b–10
Psalm 149:1b–2,3–4,5–6a and 9b
Matthew 23:13–22

AUGUST 26

*With such affection for you, we were determined to share with you
not only the Gospel of God, but our very selves as well,
so dearly beloved had you become to us.*
—1 THESSALONIANS 2:8

This is the heart of ministry, to share our very selves with
others. We share ourselves with people who become beloved
to us. Thus, ministry is generated by love, not a sense of duty
or righteousness. When I consider participating in a ministry,
I should assess how much I truly care for those it serves.
More than that, am I willing to grow in my love?

1 Thessalonians 2:1–8
Psalm 139:1–3,4–6
Matthew 23:23–26

AUGUST 27

• ST. MONICA •

Jesus said,
"Woe to you, scribes and Pharisees, you hypocrites.
You are like whitewashed tombs, which appear beautiful on the outside,
but inside are full of dead men's bones and every kind of filth."
—MATTHEW 23:27

Jesus was not easy on people who did not have integrity—who were not the same on the inside as on the outside. He requires honesty, consistency between who we really are and how we appear to others. He would rather we be honest about our sins and shortcomings. At least then, we are working in reality rather than falsehood.

1 Thessalonians 2:9–13
Psalm 139:7–8,9–10,11–12ab
Matthew 23:27–32

AUGUST 28

*Teach us to number our days aright,
that we may gain wisdom of heart.*
—PSALM 90:12

During my forties, I spent about a year contemplating my
own death. This helped me sort out my priorities. It was a
form of "numbering" my days. If, every day, you consider that
it may be your last, you tend to let go of what is
unimportant. Such a practice can develop everyday wisdom.

Friday

AUGUST 29

• THE PASSION OF ST. JOHN THE BAPTIST •

Herod feared John, knowing him to be a righteous and holy man,
and kept him in custody.
When he heard him speak he was very much perplexed,
yet he liked to listen to him.

—MARK 6:20

Herod feared John, recognized his righteousness, even
enjoyed listening to him. But when given a choice, Herod
put John to death. It's rather frightening how much we can
be attracted to holiness without actually following a holy
way of life. What counts is how we live right now.

1 Thessalonians 4:1–8 (429)
Psalm 97:1 and 2b,5–6,10,11–12
Mark 6:17–29 (634)

AUGUST 30

Then the one who had received the one talent came forward and said,
"Master, I knew you were a demanding person,
harvesting where you did not plant
and gathering where you did not scatter;
so out of fear I went off and buried your talent in the ground.
Here it is back."
—MATTHEW 25:24–25

Fear can become a posture toward life. I don't want to take
any risk. I want to always feel safe. I presume that others are
out to get me, that the world will devour me if I'm not
careful. In this parable, Jesus rejects a fearful outlook. He
wants us to step out, use our gifts, such as they are.
Why should we not be fearful?
Our "master" is loving and generous.

1 Thessalonians 4:9–11
Psalm 98:1,7–8,9
Matthew 25:14–30

Sunday

AUGUST 31

The father of orphans and the defender of widows
is God in his holy dwelling.
God gives a home to the forsaken;
he leads forth prisoners to prosperity.
—PSALM 68:5–6

Do I want to be on God's side? If so, then I must be on the side of widows and orphans (the disadvantaged), the forsaken, and the incarcerated. Are such people in my life? Am I responding to their needs?

Sirach 3:17–18,20,28–29
Psalm 68:4–5,6–7,10–11
Hebrews 12:18–19,22–24a
Luke 14:1,7–14

Monday

SEPTEMBER 1

• LABOR DAY •

[Jesus said,] "Indeed, I tell you,
there were many widows in Israel in the days of Elijah
when the sky was closed for three and a half years
and a severe famine spread over the entire land.
It was to none of these that Elijah was sent,
but only to a widow in Zarephath in the land of Sidon."
—LUKE 4:25–26

Jesus is pretty daring, here, suggesting that God's favor
extends beyond the people of Israel. As a people, the
Israelites had suffered much at the hands of other armies and
cultures. They counted on God being on their side. Much as
we tend to do still. Lord, help us remember that your
compassion extends beyond borders of every kind and
to every person.

1 Thessalonians 4:13–18
Psalm 96:1 and 3,4–5,11–12,13
Luke 4:16–30

Tuesday

SEPTEMBER 2

*They were all amazed and said to one another,
"What is there about his word?
For with authority and power he commands the unclean spirits,
and they come out."
And news of him spread everywhere in the surrounding region.*
—LUKE 4:36–37

I was named after a woman who positively shone with the
Holy Spirit. Whenever I encountered her, I could not
question God's love and power. When a person operates out
of God's love and power, our spirits respond, don't they? We
recognize what cannot be hidden—at least, it cannot be
hidden from anyone willing to see. You and I can walk in
such unity with God that people respond to our presence
with joy, hope, and faith—because they are drawn to the
Holy Spirit working in us.

1 Thessalonians 5:1–6,9–11
Psalm 27:1,4,13–14
Luke 4:31–37

⇒ 276 ⇐

Of this you have already heard
through the word of truth, the Gospel, that has come to you.
Just as in the whole world it is bearing fruit and growing,
so also among you,
from the day you heard it and came to know the grace of God in truth.
—COLOSSIANS 1:5–6

God's word and truth are bearing fruit and growing "in the whole world." Do we believe this? Can we trust it? More important, can we trust—do we believe—that God is bearing fruit in our own lives? What fruit do you see in your life right now—fruit that has grown out of God's truth and word?

Colossians 1:1–8
Psalm 52:10,11
Luke 4:38–44

Thursday

SEPTEMBER 4

The LORD has made his salvation known:
in the sight of the nations he has revealed his justice.
—PSALM 98:2

If we look for God's salvation and justice, we will see them,
sometimes where we don't expect. Christian hope is all about
expecting God to show up, anytime and anywhere. Holy
Spirit, please nurture such hope in me now, and in the
coming weeks and months.

Colossians 1:9–14
Psalm 98:2–3ab,3cd–4,5–6
Luke 5:1–11

For in [Jesus] were created all things in heaven and on earth,
the visible and the invisible,
whether thrones or dominions or principalities or powers;
all things were created through him and for him.
—COLOSSIANS 1:16

It's clear that Jesus had a part in creating all things, including mysteries beyond our understanding. We have no reason to fear the unknown because all is known by him. It is foolish to obsess about what is mysterious and hidden, paranormal, and so forth. Sometimes our greatest temptation is to long for knowledge that has not yet been revealed to us. Rather, we can live in faith, patiently, until Jesus gives us the understanding when we're ready.

Colossians 1:15–20
Psalm 100:1b–2,3,4,5
Luke 5:33–39

Saturday

SEPTEMBER 6

While Jesus was going through a field of grain on a sabbath,
his disciples were picking the heads of grain,
rubbing them in their hands, and eating them.
—LUKE 6:1

This detail about the disciples is mentioned, I'm sure, because
of what immediately follows: Pharisees questioning their
"working" on the Sabbath by "harvesting" grain. But I love
this because it shows us a group of people, followers of Jesus,
who, in the midst of ministry, get hungry. Their only option
is to pluck a few grains of wheat as they go. Every day, the
disciples and friends of Jesus had to deal with life as it is:
hunger, needing a place to sleep, shelter from weather. They
were only human, as we are.

Colossians 1:21–23
Psalm 54:3–4,6 and 8
Luke 6:1–5

And scarce do we guess the things on earth,
and what is within our grasp we find with difficulty;
but when things are in heaven, who can search them out?
—WISDOM 9:16

It's disappointing to encounter people who are certain that everything worth knowing can be proven empirically through science. They do not accept that there might be ways of knowing beyond the scientific method, and this mindset prevents them from inviting other kinds of wisdom. We can celebrate the sciences because they are among God's greatest gifts to the human family. Along with that, may we be humble, willing to learn, open to what we do not yet see or understand.

Wisdom 9:13–18b
Psalm 90:3–4,5–6,12–13,14–17 (1)
Philemon 9–10,12–17
Luke 14:25–33

• THE NATIVITY OF THE BLESSED VIRGIN MARY •

You, Bethlehem-Ephrathah,
too small to be among the clans of Judah,
From you shall come forth for me
one who is to be ruler in Israel;
Whose origin is from of old,
from ancient time.
—MICAH 5:2

Whether the prophet's words here refer to a future king or to Jesus the Messiah, one thing is clear: God might call to greatness a person from the most insignificant family or place. God calls you and me to greatness of spirit as we learn the ways of Jesus, the path of God. It doesn't matter where we come from as long as we are willing.

Micah 5:1–4a or Romans 8:28–30
Psalm 13:6ab,6c
Matthew 1:1–16,18–23 or 1:18–23

⇒ 282 ⇐

*Everyone in the crowd sought to touch him
because power came forth from him and healed them all.*
—LUKE 6:19

I think that most of us Christians are uncomfortable with our own power. The Holy Spirit dwells within us and can move through us to touch others. There is power simply in a person's presence; my compassion, wisdom, and love can change the atmosphere in a room. Will I be bold enough to claim the power God gives me in Jesus? Am I willing to be a vessel of healing, available to others?

Colossians 2:6–15
Psalm 145:1b–2,8–9,10–11
Luke 6:12–19

Wednesday

SEPTEMBER 10

Stop lying to one another,
since you have taken off the old self with its practices
and have put on the new self,
which is being renewed, for knowledge,
in the image of its creator.
—COLOSSIANS 3:9–10

It's significant that these instructions begin with "Stop lying to one another." Untruth is at the heart of what misguides us and hurts us. What is the truth? Each person is made in God's image. Spiritual growth will guide us to that truth and compel us to act like people who are made in God's image.

Colossians 3:1–11
Psalm 145:2–3,10–11,12–13ab
Luke 6:20–26

⇒ 284 ⇐

Thursday

SEPTEMBER 11

Let the word of Christ dwell in you richly,
as in all wisdom you teach and admonish one another,
singing psalms, hymns, and spiritual songs
with gratitude in your hearts to God.
—COLOSSIANS 3:16

Teaching, admonishing, singing prayers and spiritual songs, expressing gratitude—are all these things the result of Christ dwelling in us richly? Or do we invite Christ to dwell in us richly when we do these things? This probably works both ways. Christ living in us moves us to a spiritually vital life, and our practices of spiritual vitality make within us a good home for Christ.

Colossians 3:12–17
Psalm 150:1b–2,3–4,5–6
Luke 6:27–38

⇒ 285 ⇐

I was once a blasphemer and a persecutor and an arrogant man,
but I have been mercifully treated
because I acted out of ignorance in my unbelief.
—1 TIMOTHY 1:13

The apostle Paul speaks of himself as one who persecuted
followers of Jesus. Oddly enough, Paul's heart was in the
right place, as far as he knew. He was tracking down people
whose beliefs could harm the Jewish faith Paul knew and
loved. He was full of zeal for what was righteous. Then he
encountered Christ, and this changed his understanding
completely. Paul was wise enough to admit that he'd been
wrong, if well-intentioned. Today, all people of faith need to
become this willing to see their mistakes and change course
rather than cling in arrogance to a familiar way of thinking.

1 Timothy 1:1–2,12–14
Psalm 16:1b–2a and 5,7–8,11
Luke 6:39–42

Who is like the LORD, our God,
and looks upon the heavens and the earth below?
He raises up the lowly from the dust;
from the dunghill he lifts up the poor.

—PSALM 113:6–7

Almighty God, who sees all and knows all, makes a point to raise up the lowly and lift up the poor. That should tell us something, shouldn't it? If, out of all whom God sees, the poor and lowly are people he notices, then shouldn't we do the same?

1 Timothy 1:15–17
Psalm 113:1b–2,3–4,5a and 6–7
Luke 6:43–49

"For God did not send his Son into the world to condemn the world,
but that the world might be saved through him."
—JOHN 3:17

Most people don't believe what Jesus says here in John's
Gospel. It's too easy to think of God as ready to punish the
whole world, as if Jesus came to clear up the mess we made.
But, throughout the Gospels, Jesus says little in terms of
judging us. He rarely approaches a person by first talking
about the person's sin—and in the few instances where that
happens, Jesus is addressing spiritual leaders whose sins cause
great harm to the faith of others. Mainly, you see Jesus
encountering and healing people. He came to give us
life—that was the real mission. Can you believe it?

Numbers 21:4b–9
Psalm 78:1bc–2,34–35,36–37,38
Philippians 2:6–11
John 3:13–17

SEPTEMBER 15

Simeon blessed them and said to Mary, his mother,
"Behold, this child is destined
for the fall and rise of many in Israel,
and to be a sign that will be contradicted
(and you yourself a sword will pierce)
so that the thoughts of many hearts may be revealed."
—LUKE 2:34–35

As a new mother, Mary would not have understood what Simeon was talking about. This happened a few days after Jesus' birth, before the Holy Family had to flee to Egypt so that King Herod would not kill the child. Then the years went by, and as Mary watched her son's ministry unfold, she must have recalled Simeon's words. It's possible that we will receive a message from God before we are able to comprehend it. So we tuck away the mystery and wait for God to make it clear.

1 Timothy 2:1–8 (443)
Psalm 28:2,7,8–9
John 19:25–27 or Luke 2:33–35 (639)

Tuesday

SEPTEMBER 16

• ST. CORNELIUS, POPE, AND ST. CYPRIAN, BISHOP, MARTYRS •

[Jesus] stepped forward and touched the coffin;
at this the bearers halted,
and he said, "Young man, I tell you, arise!"
The dead man sat up and began to speak,
and Jesus gave him to his mother. . . .
This report about him spread through the whole of Judea
and in all the surrounding region.
—LUKE 7:14–17

We probably underestimate the ruckus Jesus caused in the whole region where he preached, taught, and healed. Those who lived through those days with him were likely not surprised when Jesus began to be met with criticism, resistance, even hostility. He demonstrated amazing power, and crowds were drawn to him. No wonder powerful men felt threatened and eventually planned to eliminate him. Following our mission will always cost something.

1 Timothy 3:1–13
Psalm 101:1b–2ab,2cd–3ab,5,6
Luke 7:11–17

⇒ 290 ⇐

• ST. ROBERT BELLARMINE, BISHOP AND DOCTOR OF THE CHURCH •
ST. HILDEGARD OF BINGEN, VIRGIN AND DOCTOR OF THE CHURCH •

Jesus said to the crowds,
"To what shall I compare the people of this generation?
What are they like?
They are like children who sit in the marketplace and call to one another,
'We played the flute for you, but you did not dance.
We sang a dirge, but you did not weep.'"
—LUKE 7:31–32

A well-known comedian once did a riff on this: Life is
amazing, but nobody's happy. Well, Jesus made a similar
observation. He knew that no matter what he said or did,
people would find fault and invent excuses to dismiss him.
An antidote to this sort of attitude is relentless awareness and
gratitude. Lord, may we not be so impossible to please.

1 Timothy 3:14–16
Psalm 111:1–2,3–4,5–6
Luke 7:31–35

[Jesus said,] "So I tell you, her many sins have been forgiven;
hence, she has shown great love.
But the one to whom little is forgiven, loves little."
He said to her, "Your sins are forgiven."
The others at table said to themselves,
"Who is this who even forgives sins?"
But he said to the woman,
"Your faith has saved you; go in peace."
—LUKE 7:47–50

Isn't this interesting? Even sins can bring us to grace. A sin
forgiven turns into love.

1 Timothy 4:12–16
Psalm 111:7–8,9,10
Luke 7:36–50

Accompanying [Jesus] were the Twelve
and some women who had been cured of evil spirits and infirmities,
Mary, called Magdalene, from whom seven demons had gone out,
Joanna, the wife of Herod's steward Chuza,
Susanna, and many others
who provided for them out of their resources.
—LUKE 8:2–3

When God is at work, you can be sure that both men and women are involved. In the Jewish culture of Jesus' time, women were not allowed to be publicly influential. However, it was understood how influential they were in their families and extensive social networks. Here we learn that along with Jesus and the male disciples were female followers, a few of them wealthy and able to help the mission financially. I am grateful that the Gospel writer noted these details, for us to know and appreciate.

1 Timothy 6:2c–12
Psalm 49:6–7,8–10,17–18,19–20
Luke 8:1–3

• ST. ANDREW KIM TAE-GŎN, PRIEST, AND ST. PAUL CHŎNG HA-SANG,
AND COMPANIONS, MARTYRS •

Know that the LORD is God;
he made us, his we are;
his people, the flock he tends.
—PSALM 100:3

Today we remember just a few of those people who have
died for their faith. Certainly they knew that they were God's
and that no suffering, torture, or death would ever change
that. We can make a practice of remembering, especially on
the hard days, that "his we are," that we are "the flock
he tends."

1 Timothy 6:13–16
Psalm 100:1b–2,3,4,5
Luke 8:4–15

SEPTEMBER 21

Hear this, you who trample upon the needy
and destroy the poor of the land! . . .
The LORD has sworn by the pride of Jacob:
Never will I forget a thing they have done!
—AMOS 8:4,7

If you really want to know what angers God, then skim the
prophetic books in the Bible and notice how many times a
prophet chastises the people for not helping those who need
help. Injustice angers God, whose compassion is for every
person. Trampling "the needy" makes God angry. There's no
other way to interpret such words.

Amos 8:4–7
Psalm 113:1–2,4–6,7–8
1 Timothy 2:1–8
Luke 16:1–13 or 16:10–13

[Jesus said to the crowd,]
"Take care, then, how you hear.
To anyone who has, more will be given,
and from the one who has not,
even what he seems to have will be taken away."
—LUKE 8:18

Jesus has just talked about not hiding our light. We can watch people use whatever resources they have, which results in more resources, more opportunities. But those who disregard whatever light or knowledge they have become stuck, lose momentum. Jesus implies here that each person is accountable for whatever knowledge they've been given.

Ezra 1:1–6
Psalm 126:1b–2ab,2cd–3,4–5,6
Luke 8:16–18

Tuesday

SEPTEMBER 23

• ST. PIUS OF PIETRELCINA, PRIEST •

[Jesus] was told, "Your mother and your brothers are standing outside and they wish to see you."
He said to them in reply, "My mother and my brothers are those who hear the word of God and act on it."
—LUKE 8:20–21

Jesus' response in this situation would not have been well received. In the tribal culture of the time, family meant just about everything. Jesus was making a radical statement, redefining family. Family to him was anyone doing God's will. He requires that we redefine life in various ways, and the way we understand the community of God is part of that.

Ezra 6:7–8,12b,14–20
Psalm 122:1–2,3–4ab,4cd–5
Luke 8:19–21

*[Jesus said,] "And as for those who do not welcome you,
when you leave that town,
shake the dust from your feet in testimony against them."*
—LUKE 9:5

Notice that Jesus does not try to convince people or change
their minds. He instructs the disciples to leave when they are
not welcome, to shake off the dust from that place and
continue on their way. Jesus invites, but he does not coerce.
When we encounter resistance to our message, it's best to
refrain from argument and leave people to their opinions and
desires. And pray that, eventually, they will respond
to God's kindness.

Ezra 9:5–9
Tobit 13:2,3–4a,4befghn,7–8
Luke 9:1–6

Thursday

SEPTEMBER 25

Now thus says the LORD of hosts:
Consider your ways!
You have sown much, but have brought in little;
you have eaten, but have not been satisfied;
You have drunk, but have not been exhilarated;
have clothed yourselves, but not been warmed;
And whoever earned wages
earned them for a bag with holes in it.
—HAGGAI 1:5–6

The prophet seems to be asking, "How is your life working out for you?" Clearly, the people have messed-up priorities or are not living by God's way, because nothing works as it should. Sometimes we need to stop and take stock. Is life working? And if not, why not?

Haggai 1:1–8
Psalm 149:1b–2,3–4,5–6a and 9b
Luke 9:7–9

⇒ 299 ⇐

Mine is the silver and mine the gold,
says the LORD of hosts.
Greater will be the future glory of this house
than the former, says the LORD of hosts;
And in this place I will give you peace,
says the LORD of hosts.
—HAGGAI 2:8–9

Preceding this text in Haggai were comments about how the new temple could not compare to the glorious original temple in Jerusalem. But then we hear that all the riches of the world belong to God anyway. And wherever God dwells with us—in whatever sort of temple, church, or altar—because God is with us, we can know true peace.

Haggai 2:1–9
Psalm 43:1,2,3,4
Luke 9:18–22

SEPTEMBER 27

• ST. VINCENT DE PAUL, PRIEST •

See, I am coming to dwell among you, says the LORD.
Many nations shall join themselves to the LORD on that day,
and they shall be his people and he will dwell among you.
—ZECHARIAH 2:14–15

The prophet looks ahead to God's coming to live with us. He
also envisions a "people" of God that includes many nations. I
wonder what it was like for Zechariah to imagine such a
future. But we don't need to imagine it: that future is here,
with Christ's Body present here on earth and Christ's
followers represented across cultures and continents. Shall
we rejoice today that what was prophesied has come about
for us to experience?

Zechariah 2:5–9,14–15a
Jeremiah 31:10,11–12ab,13
Luke 9:43b–45

Sunday

SEPTEMBER 28

• TWENTY-SIXTH SUNDAY IN ORDINARY TIME •

[Jesus said,]
"Then Abraham said, 'If they will not listen to Moses and the prophets,
neither will they be persuaded if someone should rise from the dead.'"
—LUKE 16:31

People have various reasons for not having faith in God.
Jesus knew that for some people, all the "proof" in the world
won't make any difference. After a certain point, a person
must have an open heart. So Jesus told the parable of the
man who was sure that if his brothers heard from Abraham
himself, surely they would pay attention to God's message.
But no. There's the messenger, and the message, and then
there's the heart that is ready—or not.

Amos 6:1a,4–7
Psalm 146:7,8–9,9–10 (1b)
1 Timothy 6:11–16
Luke 16:19–31

Monday

SEPTEMBER 29

• ST. MICHAEL, ST. GABRIEL, AND ST. RAPHAEL, ARCHANGELS •

War broke out in heaven;
Michael and his angels battled against the dragon.
The dragon and its angels fought back,
but they did not prevail
and there was no longer any place for them in heaven.
—REVELATION 12:7–8

This is an ancient story; some would call it mythology. Whether or not this story happened literally, the point is clear: a great rift occurred in the universe between those beings in harmony with God and those against God. Their war set a stage for our human story. We need not be surprised that the world roils with evil and conflict. We need only determine if we desire to work with God or against God.

Daniel 7:9–10,13–14 or Revelation 12:7–12ab
Psalm 138:1–2ab,2cde–3,4–5
John 1:47–51

SEPTEMBER 30

• ST. JEROME, PRIEST AND DOCTOR OF THE CHURCH •

When the days for Jesus to be taken up were fulfilled,
he resolutely determined to journey to Jerusalem,
and he sent messengers ahead of him.
—LUKE 9:51–52

Jesus sent messengers ahead of him to Jerusalem, no doubt to arrange for lodging and meeting places. He worked with a network of people who were believers, his followers there in Jerusalem. The city would be unsafe for him because some leaders were already plotting how to kill him. So we see him moving strategically as well as prayerfully. Perhaps we should become better at both strategy and prayer as we move through life's dangers and uncertainties.

Zechariah 8:20–23
Psalm 87:1b–3,4–5,6–7
Luke 9:51–56

Wednesday

OCTOBER 1

• ST. THÉRÈSE OF THE CHILD JESUS,
VIRGIN AND DOCTOR OF THE CHURCH •

*The king granted my requests,
for the favoring hand of my God was upon me.*
—NEHEMIAH 2:8

God did a work in the king's heart so that Nehemiah and
others could do what they felt God called them to do. Never
underestimate God's willingness to help us, even through
people who would seem to be at odds with us.

Nehemiah 2:1–8
Psalm 137:1–2,3,4–5,6
Luke 9:57–62

⇒ 305 ⇐

Thursday

OCTOBER 2

• THE GUARDIAN ANGELS •

Ezra read plainly from the book of the law of God,
interpreting it so that all could understand what was read.
—NEHEMIAH 8:8

Ezra interpreted God's law for the people. We have always
needed interpreters of the sacred word. Those who think that
they are equipped to do the spiritual life on their own are badly
mistaken. God has provided teachers, counselors, preachers,
prophets, and spiritual companions. In the context of God's
community, we will learn to use God's word with wisdom.

Nehemiah 8:1–4a,5–6,7b–12
Psalm 19:8,9,10,11
Matthew 18:1–5,10

During the Babylonian captivity, the exiles prayed,
Justice is with the Lord, our God;
and we today are flushed with shame,
we men of Judah and citizens of Jerusalem,
that we, with our kings and rulers
and priests and prophets, and with our ancestors,
have sinned in the Lord's sight and disobeyed him.
—BARUCH 1:15–17

The exiles' prayer is eye-opening. They recognize that they, the citizens of Jerusalem, acted in concert with kings, rulers, priests, and prophets when they sinned against God. This is what we call communal sin, systemic sin, even corporate sin. Sin nearly always involves a community, people who look the other way rather than call out wrongdoing, people who encourage the wrong action. How does your community influence you?

Baruch 1:15–22
Psalm 79:1b–2,3–5,8,9
Luke 10:13–16

Saturday

OCTOBER 4

• ST. FRANCIS OF ASSISI •

For you provoked your Maker
with sacrifices to demons, to no-gods;
You forsook the Eternal God who nourished you,
and you grieved Jerusalem who fostered you.
—BARUCH 4:7–8

St. Francis of Assisi is known for his holy relationship with nature. Yet he never lost sight of the God who created it all. Francis's love for God enabled him to live in beautiful communion with the natural world. Other people through the centuries forgot the Source and turned to "no-gods" such as animals, stones, and trees. May our wonder at nature always connect us more closely to the Creator.

Baruch 4:5–12,27–29
Psalm 69:33–35,36–37
Luke 10:17–24

Sunday

OCTOBER 5

For the vision still has its time,
presses on to fulfillment, and will not disappoint;
if it delays, wait for it,
it will surely come, it will not be late.
—HABAKKUK 2:3

Lord God, may we trust in the vision you give to us, knowing
that your will for us will find its fulfillment, and at the
best time.

Habakkuk 1:2–3; 2:2–4
Psalm 95:1–2,6–7,8–9 (8)
2 Timothy 1:6–8,13–14
Luke 17:5–10

[Jesus said,] "Which of these three, in your opinion,
was neighbor to the robbers' victim?"
He answered, "The one who treated him with mercy."
Jesus said to him, "Go and do likewise."
—LUKE 10:36–37

It's so easy to get involved in theological debate rather than simply do what is right. I believe that Jesus says to us today, Pay attention to the need that is right in front of you, and you'll be fine.

Jonah 1:1—2:2, 11
Jonah 2:3,4,5,8
Luke 10:25–37

Tuesday

OCTOBER 7

• OUR LADY OF THE ROSARY •

Jesus entered a village
where a woman whose name was Martha welcomed him.
—LUKE 10:38

Let's linger with this sentence. Martha welcomed Jesus.
Perhaps she was the elder sister, even the homeowner. If
Martha welcomed Jesus, then it's a safe bet that she was
practiced at showing hospitality. I like to imagine that
Martha's home was sort of a grand central station in her
neighborhood, the place people could go to find a meal,
warmth, a listening ear. Martha's love began with
simple hospitality.

Jonah 3:1–10
Psalm 130:1b–2,3–4ab,7–8
Luke 10:38–42

OCTOBER 8

*Jonah was greatly displeased
and became angry that God did not carry out the evil
he threatened against Nineveh.*

—JONAH 4:1

Have you ever become angry when some wrongdoer didn't get what was coming to him? Well, you would understand Jonah, then. God sent him to warn Nineveh to repent, but Nineveh was an enemy of the Israelites, and Jonah would have been happy if God had destroyed the whole place. You and I have received God's mercy; why do we resist when God shows mercy to others?

Jonah 4:1–11
Psalm 86:3–4,5–6,9–10
Luke 11:1–4

Thursday

OCTOBER 9

Then you will again see the distinction
between the just and the wicked;
Between the one who serves God,
and the one who does not serve him.
—MALACHI 3:18

Just and *justice* show up a lot in the writings of the prophets.
As far as God is concerned, the one who serves God's way is
the one who is just. The person who is not just has put
herself in the category of wicked. Pretty plain language. May
God show each of us how to do justice this day.

Malachi 3:13–20b
Psalm 1:1–2,3,4 and 6
Luke 11:5–13

OCTOBER 10

The nations are sunk in the pit they have made;
in the snare they set, their foot is caught.
—PSALM 9:15

The psalmist was wise enough to recognize how the world works. So often, we are hurt as the result of our own scheming. It's not difficult to see how nations also set the stage for calamity when they act in greed and self-interest.

Some of the leaders whose evil led to current world situations were supported by the USA decades ago because it seemed in our country's best interest. The psalmist describes an ongoing dynamic. Are we willing to go the better way?

Joel 1:13–15; 2:1–2
Psalm 9:2–3,6 and 16,8–9
Luke 11:15–26

OCTOBER 11

Light dawns for the just;
and gladness, for the upright of heart.
Be glad in the LORD, you just,
and give thanks to his holy name.
—PSALM 97:11–12

When we live according to God's ways—with just and upright hearts—we will indeed see the light and know gladness. Sometimes we forget this and allow despair and cynicism to creep in. Sometimes it seems that all the good results go to those who bully and dominate the rest of us. Hold fast to the Lord's way, and watch expectantly for its good fruits.

Joel 4:12–21
Psalm 97:1–2,5–6,11–12
Luke 11:27–28

Sunday

OCTOBER 12

When [Jesus] saw them, he said,
"Go show yourselves to the priests."
As they were going they were cleansed.
—LUKE 17:14

Jesus healed people, but in most cases, he required the
person's collaboration. "Pick up your mat and walk" or
"Stretch out your hand." In this case, "Go show yourselves to
the priests," which was the standard protocol; the priest
would examine the person to validate the healing. *As the lepers*
were on their way to see the priest, their healing occurred.
When we ask God for help, we are also asking, "Lord, what
do you want me to do?"

2 Kings 5:14–17
Psalm 98:1,2–3,3–4
2 Timothy 2:8–13
Luke 17:11–19

*The Gospel about his Son, descended
from David according to the flesh,
but established as Son of God in power
according to the Spirit of holiness
through resurrection from the dead,
Jesus Christ our Lord.*
—ROMANS 1:3–4

Jesus belonged to two realms, the realm of fleshly humanity
and that of the Spirit. In some mysterious way, Jesus' death
and resurrection brought these realms together. Now we
need not consider them as separate worlds but as one holy
universe in ongoing reconciliation. Can you think of yourself
not as human and spirit but simply as one of God's beloved?

Romans 1:1–7
Psalm 98:1,2–3ab,3cd–4
Luke 11:29–32

OCTOBER 14

Ever since the creation of the world,
his invisible attributes of eternal power and divinity
have been able to be understood and perceived in what he has made.
—ROMANS 1:20

Creation speaks to us of God, if we are willing to perceive
the truth and acknowledge it. The starry sky, the immensity
of an ocean, the mysteries of bees and bison—all call us to
look beyond ourselves. May we be humble enough to call
that beyond-ness God, and to respond to the power and
divinity with gratitude and wonder.

Romans 1:16–25
Psalm 19:2–3,4–5
Luke 11:37–41

And [Jesus] said, "Woe also to you scholars of the law!
You impose on people burdens hard to carry,
but you yourselves do not lift one finger to touch them."
—LUKE 11:46

It's dangerous to become teachers because people might
actually try to do what we say. People might accept our
words as truth. I've been speaking in front of groups for
years, and I always tremble at the thought of how much
influence I have. I hope to always sense how much
responsibility I bear because of my position as speaker,
teacher, or retreat leader. Those of us who teach must take
care to do, ourselves, what we invite others to do.

Romans 2:1–11
Psalm 62:2–3,6–7,9
Luke 11:42–46

OCTOBER 16

Now the righteousness of God has been manifested apart from the law,
though testified to by the law and the prophets,
the righteousness of God through faith in Jesus Christ
for all who believe.
—ROMANS 3:21–22

The law, as given to the Israelites, had a clear purpose. Yet God's presence and character speak for themselves, with or without a law. Beyond our religious systems lies a truth that is expansive and deep, and those who long for the Holy will perceive the truth and take joy in it.

Romans 3:21–30
Psalm 130:1b–2, 3–4, 5–6ab
Luke 11:47–54

Friday

OCTOBER 17

• ST. IGNATIUS OF ANTIOCH, BISHOP AND MARTYR •

Blessed is he whose fault is taken away,
whose sin is covered.
Blessed the man to whom the LORD imputes not guilt,
in whose spirit there is no guile.
—PSALM 32:1B–2

It's astonishing that the psalmist—centuries before Jesus arrived to proclaim the Good News—had such a strong sense of God's compassion. Yes, the early Israelites had the Law and the Prophets, who often spoke of God's mercy. But this psalm describes complete confidence in God's willingness to put away our guilt completely. Why, then, do I allow myself to be burdened with guilt that, in God's mind, no longer exists?

Romans 4:1–8
Psalm 32:1b–2,5,11
Luke 12:1–7

⇒ 321 ⇐

Saturday

OCTOBER 18

• ST. LUKE, EVANGELIST •

The Lord Jesus appointed seventy-two disciples
whom he sent ahead of him in pairs
to every town and place he intended to visit.
—LUKE 10:1

It's quite stunning how much Jesus trusted the disciples to go ahead of him and make the initial encounters with people of the towns. He sent them with a few instructions, but he left much to their own judgment. Is it possible that Jesus invites us to go ahead of him, day after day, making connections with people that will help prepare them to meet him in person?

2 Timothy 4:10–17b
Psalm 145:10–11,12–13,17–18
Luke 10:1–9

Sunday

OCTOBER 19

• TWENTY-NINTH SUNDAY IN ORDINARY TIME •

I charge you in the presence of God and of Christ Jesus,
who will judge the living and the dead,
and by his appearing and his kingly power:
proclaim the word;
be persistent whether it is convenient or inconvenient;
convince, reprimand, encourage through all patience and teaching.
—2 TIMOTHY 4:1–2

May we remember this: it is rarely convenient to speak the truth or to treat others as God desires they be treated. The work of God will mess up our plans and upend our ideas. But it is the work of eternal love.

Exodus 17:8–13
Psalm 121:1–2,3–4,5–6,7–8
2 Timothy 3:14—4:2
Luke 18:1–8

⇒ 323 ⇐

Monday

OCTOBER 20

• ST. PAUL OF THE CROSS, PRIEST •

Someone in the crowd said to Jesus,
"Teacher, tell my brother to share the inheritance with me."
He replied to him,
"Friend, who appointed me as your judge and arbitrator?"
—LUKE 12:13–14

Don't you know that people probably approached Jesus with all sorts of problems? That they assumed he would untangle their legal troubles and scold those who bothered them? But he knew that until people were renewed within, the same problems would crop up again and again. This passage doesn't give us an excuse to ignore others' practical needs, but it reminds us of the ultimate purpose: to see people made new in Christ.

Romans 4:20–25
Luke 1:69–70,71–72,73–75
Luke 12:13–21

OCTOBER 21

Jesus said to his disciples,
"Gird your loins and light your lamps
and be like servants who await their master's return from a wedding,
ready to open immediately when he comes and knocks."
—LUKE 12:35

Jesus speaks with urgency here. We're to be ready, but for what? To hear God's call. To speak the truth. To suffer for the right reasons. To aid those in need. To bring God's new order to life at a moment's notice.

Romans 5:12,15b,17–19,20b–21
Psalm 40:7–8a,8b–9,10,17
Luke 12:35–38

Wednesday

OCTOBER 22

• ST. JOHN PAUL II, POPE •

Do you not know that if you present yourselves
to someone as obedient slaves,
you are slaves of the one you obey,
either of sin, which leads to death,
or of obedience, which leads to righteousness?
—ROMANS 6:16

Paul uses the quite familiar example of slavery to emphasize that, one way or another, we "serve" something or someone. Whom or what we serve will determine our priorities, our actions, our attitudes, and the end result. Why not serve the One who gives us mercy, forgiveness, life? And, as we know from Jesus' words, we are not servants but adopted daughters and sons. We are not slaves but God's beloved.

Romans 6:12–18
Psalm 124:1b–3,4–6,7–8
Luke 12:39–48

Thursday

OCTOBER 23

• ST. JOHN OF CAPISTRANO, PRIEST •

The wages of sin is death,
but the gift of God is eternal life in Christ Jesus our Lord.
—ROMANS 6:23

This verse is quoted frequently, but too often we forget to live as if it's true. God offers us life in Christ Jesus. There's nothing we can do to earn or achieve this life, but God does not force us to reach out and embrace it. What would today look like if I embrace with gratitude and joy this life to which God invites me?

Romans 6:19–23
Psalm 1:1–2,3,4 and 6
Luke 12:49–53

Friday

OCTOBER 24

• ST. ANTHONY MARY CLARET, BISHOP •

[Jesus said,]
"You know how to interpret the appearance of the earth and the sky;
why do you not know how to interpret the present time?"
—LUKE 12:56

I'm sure Jesus would ask us this same question today. We predict the weather, the economic market, and who will win the playoffs. We plan our lives in five- and ten-year increments. Yet our spiritual sensibilities are dulled to what is happening within people and how that plays out in society. Lord, teach us to pay attention to the heart and soul of our communities and respond as you guide us.

Romans 7:18–25a
Psalm 119:66,68,76,77,93,94
Luke 12:54–59

Saturday

OCTOBER 25

Some people told Jesus about the Galileans
whose blood Pilate had mingled with the blood of their sacrifices.
He said to them in reply,
"Do you think that because these Galileans suffered in this way
they were greater sinners than all other Galileans?
By no means!"
—LUKE 13:1–2

Jesus makes two points in this Luke passage. One, a person's
suffering is not necessarily a direct consequence of sin.
Two—and this is covered in the rest of the passage, not
quoted above—everyone should be wary, because if we don't
all change our hearts and our ways, destruction and calamity
will keep happening. He implies what we sometimes call
communal, or corporate, sin: sinful processes and structures
that endanger everyone.

Romans 8:1–11
Psalm 24:1b–2,3–4ab,5–6
Luke 13:1–9

OCTOBER 26

• THIRTIETH SUNDAY IN ORDINARY TIME •

The LORD is a God of justice,
who knows no favorites.
Though not unduly partial toward the weak,
yet he hears the cry of the oppressed.
The Lord is not deaf to the wail of the orphan,
nor to the widow when she pours out her complaint.
—SIRACH 35:16–17

In these days of grave political strife, we must remember that God is a God of justice and that the oppressed, orphans, and widows have God's ear. When any society turns a blind eye to the suffering of its people, it has left the path of holiness.

Sirach 35:12–14,16–18
Psalm 34:2–3,17–18,19,23 (7a)
2 Timothy 4:6–8,16–18
Luke 18:9–14

OCTOBER 27

[Jesus] laid hands on her,
and she at once stood up straight and glorified God.
But the leader of the synagogue,
indignant that Jesus had cured on the sabbath,
said to the crowd in reply,
"There are six days when work should be done.
Come on those days to be cured, not on the sabbath day."
—LUKE 13:13–14

So, what kind of a "leader" begrudges a suffering person to be healed, whatever day it is? The synagogue leader reveals through his words the hardness of his heart. Whenever we value anything—even religious rules—more important than human life, we have fallen into idolatry.

Romans 8:12–17
Psalm 68:2 and 4,6–7ab,20–21
Luke 13:10–17

OCTOBER 28

• ST. SIMON AND ST. JUDE, APOSTLES •

You are no longer strangers and sojourners,
but you are fellow citizens with the holy ones
and members of the household of God.
—EPHESIANS 2:19

The theme of belonging rings throughout God's word. We belong. We are welcome. We have a family, a community, a household. And all of it exists in the mystical and wonderful realm of what is holy. May we remember this when we greet fellow parishioners, when we stand in church and sing, when we partake of the Eucharist. We are living a miracle.

Ephesians 2:19–22
Psalm 19:2–3,4–5
Luke 6:12–16

*The one who searches hearts
knows what is the intention of the Spirit,
because he intercedes for the holy ones
according to God's will.*
—ROMANS 8:27

The Holy Spirit, who dwells within us, is in constant communion with our spirits. In the deepest, truest part of ourselves, this holy conversation is going on. Part of our own maturation process is our growing awareness of this rich life within. As we become more sensitive to the Spirit, we will naturally follow the best way, and fulfill God's loving desires for us.

Romans 8:26–30
Psalm 13:4–5,6
Luke 13:22–30

OCTOBER 30

If God is for us, who can be against us?
He who did not spare his own Son
but handed him over for us all,
how will he not also give us everything else along with him?
—ROMANS 8:31–32

Do you generally think of God of the Universe as being *for* you? I hope so. I hope it occurs to you at least once a day that the Creator of all is on your side, is rooting for you to do well and grow in wisdom and in grace.

Romans 8:31b–39
Psalm 109:21–22,26–27,30–31
Luke 13:31–35

Friday

OCTOBER 31

*On a sabbath Jesus went to dine
at the home of one of the leading Pharisees,
and the people there were observing him carefully.*
—LUKE 14:1

During his public ministry, Jesus was always "on." People
were around him constantly, including critics ready to
question and judge everything he said and did. How did he
manage such pressure? He spent time with the Father in
prayer. He worked with the Father and listened to the Father.
Also, Jesus knew the Scriptures very well. Thus, his public
life was founded upon wisdom and the ongoing
companionship of Jesus' heavenly Father.

Romans 9:1–5
Psalm 147:12–13,14–15,19–20
Luke 14:1–6

⋟ 335 ⋞

[Jesus said,] "Blessed are they who hunger and thirst for righteousness,
for they will be satisfied."
—MATTHEW 5:6

Never mind if people call you an idealist. Keep hungering
and thirsting for righteousness. Jesus calls you blessed. Not
only that, he also assures you that you will be satisfied. Our
hunger matters. Our desire for good joins the holy energy of
God, and good results will come.

Revelation 7:2–4,9–14
Psalm 24:1b–2,3–4ab,5–6
1 John 3:1–3
Matthew 5:1–12a

Sunday

NOVEMBER 2

• THE COMMEMORATION OF ALL THE FAITHFUL DEPARTED
(ALL SOULS' DAY) •

Those who trust in him shall understand truth,
and the faithful shall abide with him in love:
because grace and mercy are with his holy ones,
and his care is with his elect.

—WISDOM 3:9

This proverb describes the person who follows after God,
who sticks with the Holy One, who abides upon the path of
good. Allow this to be your prayer today, as you endure in
this graced life of faith.

Wisdom 3:1–9
Psalm 25:6 and 7b, 17–18,20–21
Romans 5:5–11 or 6:3–9
John 6:37–40
Other readings may be selected.

Monday

NOVEMBER 3

• ST. MARTIN DE PORRES, RELIGIOUS •

"See, you lowly ones, and be glad;
you who seek God, may your hearts revive!
For the LORD hears the poor,
and his own who are in bonds he spurns not."
—PSALM 69:33–34

Various times the prophets and ancient writers tell us that
God hears the poor. The psalmist encourages "lowly
ones"—those with no power or voice—to be glad. Let's help
one another revive hearts to continue seeking God through
all events, trials, puzzles, and circumstances.

Romans 11:29–36
Psalm 69:30–31,33–34,36
Luke 14:12–14

Tuesday

NOVEMBER 4

• ST. CHARLES BORROMEO, BISHOP •

Rejoice in hope,
endure in affliction,
persevere in prayer.
—ROMANS 12:12

The writer of the letter to the Christians in Rome assumes
that they face affliction; he tells the people to endure. But
not simply endure: rejoice because they have hope. And
never, ever stop praying. I can honestly say that I've had to
deal with very little affliction, and yet I become discouraged
so easily. Lord, engrave these words upon my heart
and mind.

Romans 12:5–16ab
Psalm 131:1bcde,2,3
Luke 14:15–24

NOVEMBER 5

Great crowds were traveling with Jesus,
and he turned and addressed them,
"If anyone comes to me without hating his father and mother,
wife and children, brothers and sisters,
and even his own life,
he cannot be my disciple."
—LUKE 14:25–26

Okay, it seems that Jesus decided to thin the crowd. Just as he seemed to be where any speaker or teacher wants to be—in front of many, many listeners—Jesus gave them a reality check. His words are hard even for the most dedicated disciple, but they certainly would have stopped people who followed him merely because they wanted to see miracles or because following Jesus was the current trend. It does little good to encourage people to a life they do not yet want or are not ready for.

Romans 13:8–10
Psalm 112:1b–2,4–5,9
Luke 14:25–33

Thursday

NOVEMBER 6

For if we live, we live for the Lord,
and if we die, we die for the Lord;
so then, whether we live or die, we are the Lord's.
For this is why Christ died and came to life,
that he might be Lord of both the dead and the living.
—ROMANS 14:7–9

I don't fully understand the message of these verses. Jesus' life, death, and resurrection caused a monumental shift in the universe. In becoming Lord over the dead as well as the living, he stretched his love and influence beyond earthly human existence. All I can do is wonder and remain in awe. And give thanks. And, probably, I should not fear death anymore.

Romans 14:7–12
Psalm 27:1bcde,4,13–14
Luke 15:1–10

≽ 341 ≼

Friday

NOVEMBER 7

In Christ Jesus, then, I have reason to boast in what pertains to God.
—ROMANS 15:17

When I speak in front of groups these days—at events having to do with faith or prayer—I talk about spiritual confidence. This is what Paul referred to in this verse. His confidence was in the work and character of God. Paul could be confident because, in Christ, he collaborated with God. I long for all followers of Jesus to become joyfully confident in who we are and what we can do, because God has transformed us with love and grace.

Romans 15:14–21
Psalm 98:1,2–3ab,3cd–4
Luke 16:1–8

NOVEMBER 8

[Jesus] said to them,
*"You justify yourselves in the sight of others,
but God knows your hearts;
for what is of human esteem is an abomination in the sight of God."*
—LUKE 16:15

God knows my heart. God knows the heart of the person who seems out to get me. God knows the heart of the person whose approval I seek. God knows the heart of those who pray for me. It should be enough for me that God knows every heart. This saves me the trouble of trying to judge others, which I have no capacity to do anyway. Rather than try to assess others' hearts, I hope to tend my own heart more consistently.

Romans 16:3–9,16,22–27
Psalm 145:2–3,4–5,10–11
Luke 16:9–15

NOVEMBER 9

• THE DEDICATION OF THE LATERAN BASILICA •

There is a stream whose runlets gladden the city of God,
the holy dwelling of the Most High.
God is in its midst; it shall not be disturbed;
God will help it at the break of dawn.

—PSALM 46:4–5

The metaphor of fresh, full, flowing streams appears again
and again in Scripture. Those of us who can get fresh water
by turning on a faucet don't really understand how important
a good stream is. It brings life, it sustains life. It can refresh,
and it can cleanse. Would it help our prayer this week to
imagine ourselves standing in a fresh stream that overflows
with God's love?

Ezekiel 47:1–2,8–9,12
Psalm 46:2–3,5–6,8–9
1 Corinthians 3:9c–11,16–17
John 2:13–22

Because into a soul that plots evil, wisdom enters not,
nor dwells she in a body under debt of sin.
—WISDOM 1:4

We talk a lot about people who are greatly gifted and highly intelligent and astonishingly successful. But we don't hear much about wisdom. Wisdom was personified in various Scriptures as an aspect of the deity, an integral part of God's holiness and righteousness. A smart person might walk into sin despite her intelligence, but a wise person will see a wrong path for what it is. Lord God, we ask you for wisdom to dwell within us, to nurture and guide us.

Wisdom 1:1–7
Psalm 139:1b–3,4–6,7–8,9–10
Luke 17:1–6

God formed man to be imperishable;
the image of his own nature he made them.
But by the envy of the Devil, death entered the world,
and they who are in his possession experience it.
—WISDOM 2:23–24

This is an interesting thought: the devil envied *us*, human beings. Because we are eternal and made in God's image, we became the target of God's enemy. It seems that the devil understands better who we are than we do! Do we appreciate how marvelous it is to bear the image of the Divine? Do we care for our lives because they are more precious than any riches in the world?

Wisdom 2:23—3:9
Psalm 34:2–3,16–17,18–19
Luke 17:7–10

Wednesday

NOVEMBER 12

• ST. JOSAPHAT, BISHOP AND MARTYR •

For the Lord of all shows no partiality,
nor does he fear greatness,
Because he himself made the great as well as the small,
and he provides for all alike;
but for those in power a rigorous scrutiny impends.
—WISDOM 6:7–8

When I observe the evil unleashed upon nations—war and
carnage issuing from greed and hunger for power—I think of
the leaders who could do the right thing but don't. Indeed,
God will hold responsible those who had power and
greatness in this world but who used them unwisely.
Whatever power we have must be used to create the world
God desires.

Wisdom 6:1–11
Psalm 82:3–4,6–7
Luke 17:11–19

Thursday

NOVEMBER 13

• ST. FRANCES XAVIER CABRINI, VIRGIN •

Asked by the Pharisees when the Kingdom of God would come,
Jesus said in reply,
"The coming of the Kingdom of God cannot be observed,
and no one will announce, 'Look, here it is,' or, 'There it is.'
For behold, the Kingdom of God is among you."
—LUKE 17:20–21

Jesus came to dwell among us, and his consistent message
was this: *The kingdom of God is here.* Yes, it's here. The kingdom
exists wherever people live out their divine purpose. When
we love God with everything we have and love our
neighbors as ourselves, we bring to life, every moment and
every day, the kingdom of God. Can you see the kingdom
manifesting around you as you love others?

Wisdom 7:22b—8:1
Psalm 119:89,90,91,130,135,175
Luke 17:20–25

NOVEMBER 14

*If they so far succeeded in knowledge
that they could speculate about the world,
how did they not more quickly find its Lord?*
—WISDOM 13:9

In various Scriptures we are told that God's presence is evident. What keeps us from perceiving this? Is it resistance or fear or pride? Is it our own insistence that we be able to explain and understand God in a scientific, empirical way, even though wise people for millennia have understood that some knowing happens in a deeper, mysterious place? The real question for me today is, Am I happy to recognize God all around me? Or do I try, for some reason, to disregard God's presence?

Wisdom 13:1–9
Psalm 19:2–3,4–5ab
Luke 17:26–37

The cloud overshadowed their camp;
and out of what had before been water, dry land was seen emerging:
Out of the Red Sea an unimpeded road,
and a grassy plain out of the mighty flood.
—WISDOM 18:17

When I cannot see a way forward, I try to remember
Scriptures such as this one. God made a way where none
was. I may not fathom how to solve this problem. I might not
have any idea what my next step should be. But the God who
brought a grassy plain out of a mighty flood can certainly
open a way this day that is right for me. Thank you!

Wisdom 18:14–16; 19:6–9
Psalm 105:2–3,36–37,42–43
Luke 18:1–8

Sunday

NOVEMBER 16

• THIRTY-THIRD SUNDAY IN ORDINARY TIME •

Lo, the day is coming, blazing like an oven,
when all the proud and all evildoers will be stubble,
and the day that is coming will set them on fire,
leaving them neither root nor branch,
says the LORD of hosts.
But for you who fear my name, there will arise
the sun of justice with its healing rays.
—MALACHI 3:19–20A

God's visitation is a fire of destruction for wickedness, but the same events shine like the sun, bringing justice and healing for those who look to God and seek to live in faith. We might call this a sort of creative destruction: in order for a new world to be formed, old systems must be dismantled. May we not fear God's creation in us. May we welcome the destruction that leads to new life.

Malachi 3:19–20a
Psalm 98:5–6,7–8,9
2 Thessalonians 3:7–12
Luke 21:5–19

He shouted, "Jesus, Son of David, have pity on me!"
The people walking in front rebuked him,
telling him to be silent,
but he kept calling out all the more,
"Son of David, have pity on me!"
—LUKE 18:38–39

This story breaks my heart because it is so typical. The needy cry out, and others hiss, "Be quiet!" We don't want to see others' needs and wounds—we wish they'd just get out of the way so that we don't have to see them. We shame and blame the victim. Evidently, people did the same back in Jesus' day. Fortunately, Jesus focused on the victim. Jesus saw him, talked with him, and helped him.

1 Maccabees 1:10–15,41–43,54–57,62–63
Psalm 119:53,61,134,150,155,158
Luke 18:35–43

Tuesday

NOVEMBER 18

• THE DEDICATION OF THE BASILICAS OF ST. PETER AND ST. PAUL, APOSTLES
• ST. ROSE PHILIPPINE DUCHESNE, VIRGIN •

"Therefore, by manfully giving up my life now,
I will prove myself worthy of my old age,
and I will leave to the young a noble example
of how to die willingly and generously
for the revered and holy laws."
—2 MACCABEES 6:27–28

These are the words of a Jewish elder who was executed
because he would not deny his faith. It is possible to die
"willingly and generously." Am I prepared to be so free? Am I
consistent in my loyalty to the God I know who has loved
me from the beginning?

2 Maccabees 6:18–31 or Acts 28:11–16,30–31
Psalm 3:2–3,4–5,6–7 or 98:1,2–3ab,3cd–4,5–6
Luke 19:1–10 or Matthew 14:22–33

⋟ 353 ⋞

"I beg you, child, to look at the heavens and the earth
and see all that is in them;
then you will know that God did not make them out of existing things;
and in the same way the human race came into existence.
Do not be afraid of this executioner."
—2 MACCABEES 7:28–29

Here's the story of another martyr and the mother who
encourages him to stay true to himself, his God, and his
people. She asks that he expand his gaze to the universe to
remind himself that the God who created everything from
nothing would also be with him. In times of distress, it can
help to stand back, take a deep breath, open our hearts, and
widen our viewpoint.

2 Maccabees 7:1,20–31
Psalm 17:1bcd,5–6,8b and 15
Luke 19:11–28

Thursday

NOVEMBER 20

*Many who sought to live according
to righteousness and religious custom
went out into the desert to settle there.*
—1 MACCABEES 2:29

At several points in history, people who wanted to live true
to their faith left home to find a wilderness in which to live
and pray. It's all right to retreat. Sometimes we need a safe,
quiet place in which to rest, regroup, and soak up the silence.
Sometimes we must leave our home, job, community,
responsibilities, and relationships for a time of healing and
prayer. This has been true for thousands of years. Welcome
the wisdom of retreat.

1 Maccabees 2:15–29
Psalm 50:1b–2,5–6,14–15
Luke 19:41–44

Friday

NOVEMBER 21

• THE PRESENTATION OF THE BLESSED VIRGIN MARY •

*Jesus entered the temple area and proceeded to drive out
those who were selling things, saying to them,*
"It is written, My house shall be a house of prayer,
but you have made it a den of thieves."
And every day he was teaching in the temple area.
—LUKE 19:45

It's interesting that after the disturbance Jesus caused among
the temple vendors, there were still plenty of people who
wanted to hear him teach. I suspect that many of the
ordinary folks were hungry to hear Jesus, whereas the
businessmen and religious leaders were less willing to
consider what he had to say. Perhaps those with money and
position felt no need for teaching or preaching. Perhaps they
had more to lose if people paid attention to what Jesus had to
say. It's wise to notice who resists change, and why.

1 Maccabees 4:36–37,52–59
1 Chronicles 29:10bcd,11abc,11d–12a,12bcd
Luke 19:45–48

⇒ 356 ⇐

[Jesus said,] "The children of this age marry and remarry;
but those who are deemed worthy to attain to the coming age
and to the resurrection of the dead
neither marry nor are given in marriage.
They can no longer die,
for they are like angels;
and they are the children of God
because they are the ones who will rise."
—LUKE 20:34–36

What a mystery Jesus speaks of! He refers to a time/place/
state in which people will exist but differently. These are the
ones called the children of God. These are the ones who will
rise. Jesus speaks of resurrection, of existence beyond our
present state. He is talking with learned men, who are left
with nothing to say. We can gain much hope from this
conversation, can't we?

1 Maccabees 6:1–13
Psalm 9:2–3,4 and 6,16 and 19
Luke 20:27–40

NOVEMBER 23

Brothers and sisters:
Let us give thanks to the Father,
who has made you fit to share
in the inheritance of the holy ones in light.
He delivered us from the power of darkness
and transferred us to the kingdom of his beloved Son,
in whom we have redemption, the forgiveness of sins.
—COLOSSIANS 1:12–14

The writer of Colossians was an expert at painting the big picture. We believers are made heirs to God's wonders; we have been delivered from one way of being to another, vastly different, way of being. Whenever life feels like drudgery, when my faith feels faint, reading this description can provide my soul a hearty boost.

2 Samuel 5:1–3
Psalm 122:1–2,3–4,4–5
Colossians 1:12–20
Luke 23:35–43

Monday

NOVEMBER 24

• ST. ANDREW DŨNG-LẠC, PRIEST, AND COMPANIONS, MARTYRS •

To these four young men God gave knowledge and proficiency
in all literature and science,
and to Daniel the understanding of all visions and dreams.
—DANIEL 1:17

God made these young Hebrews excellent learners and not
simply in religious matters. It saddens me when Christians
minimize what's going on out in the world—in the arts and
sciences, for instance. God wants us to be fluent in the
various aspects of culture. As we try to communicate the
Good News of Jesus, we can use every "language" at our
disposal, whether poetry, astronomy, cooking, or
public policy.

Daniel 1:1–6,8–20
Daniel 3:52,53,54,55,56
Luke 21:1–4

⇒ 359 ⇐

NOVEMBER 25

• ST. CATHERINE OF ALEXANDRIA, VIRGIN AND MARTYR •

Jesus said, "All that you see here—
the days will come when there will not be left
a stone upon another stone that will not be thrown down."
—LUKE 21:6

Jesus could look ahead and see the destruction of Jerusalem, which did happen a few decades later. He was not interested in telling people, "Oh, everything's fine." He knew that everything is not fine, that people must be renewed in their hearts and minds. He also knew that every generation must live through trials and disasters. He did not encourage anyone to expect a trouble-free life. Rather, he wanted people to turn in faith to God the Father, whatever the situation.

Daniel 2:31–45
Daniel 3:57,58,59,60,61
Luke 21:5–11

Sun and moon, bless the Lord;
praise and exalt him above all forever.
Stars of heaven, bless the Lord;
praise and exalt him above all forever.
—DANIEL 3:62–63

Here's the right idea. Rather than worship the sun, moon, and stars—which people have done throughout history—invite those entities to bless and praise the One who created them. We can engage with creation enthusiastically, but that doesn't mean that we esteem creation and rely on it as we are invited to rely on our heavenly Father. Let's sing God's praises along with the trees, water, and wind!

Daniel 5:1–6,13–14,16–17,23–28
Daniel 3:62,63,64,65,66,67
Luke 21:12–19

NOVEMBER 27

• THANKSGIVING DAY •

I give thanks to my God always on your account
for the grace of God bestowed on you in Christ Jesus,
that in him you were enriched in every way,
with all discourse and all knowledge,
as the testimony to Christ was confirmed among you,
so that you are not lacking in any spiritual gift
as you wait for the revelation of our Lord Jesus Christ.
—1 CORINTHIANS 1:4–7

In the United States, today is Thanksgiving. Along with thanking God for nation, possessions, food, and family, let's thank God for all our spiritual riches, described so well in this letter to the church in Corinth.

Daniel 6:12–28
Daniel 3:68,69,70,71,72,73,74
Luke 21:20–28

proper mass in thanksgiving to god:
Sirach 50:22–24
1 Corinthians 1:3–9
Luke 17:11–19
or, for Thanksgiving Day, any readings from
the Mass "In Thanksgiving to God"

[Jesus said,] "Heaven and earth will pass away,
but my words will not pass away."
—LUKE 21:33

I don't really like to think about heaven and earth passing
away. I'm fond of my planet home. If Jesus' words will not
pass away, then what does that mean for me? That every
word that takes root in me and bears fruit will somehow carry
my life beyond this one? That everything Jesus said will
become a reality more vivid than the reality my physical
senses now know? Lord, help me sit with these words and
find comfort in them.

Daniel 7:2–14
Daniel 3:75,76,77,78,79,80,81
Luke 21:29–33

Saturday

NOVEMBER 29

Jesus said to his disciples,
"Beware that your hearts do not become drowsy
from carousing and drunkenness
and the anxieties of daily life,
and that day catch you by surprise like a trap.
For that day will assault everyone
who lives on the face of the earth."
—LUKE 21:34–35

Again and again, Jesus refers to something on its way, something that will take us by surprise if we're not careful. He speaks of a way to live that transcends just getting through the day. He warns us against a narrowing vision that focuses on daily anxieties and pleasures. He tells us repeatedly: "Pay attention." God is at work, but will we miss it because we're distracted?

Daniel 7:15–27
Daniel 3:82,83,84,85,86,87
Luke 21:34–36

NOVEMBER 30

• FIRST SUNDAY OF ADVENT •

Many people shall come and say:
"Come, let us climb the LORD's mountain,
to the house of the God of Jacob,
that he may instruct us in his ways,
and we may walk in his paths."

—ISAIAH 2:3

Can you picture a world in which people from everywhere on the globe are drawn to God's eternal family? Well, you don't have to picture it, because this is already happening. When people see God's love, compassion, and justice lived out in front of them, they are attracted to such a life. The question is, Where do they see God's way lived out, and by whom?

Isaiah 2:1–5
Psalm 122:1–2,3–4,4–5,6–7,8–9
Romans 13:11–14
Matthew 24:37–44

DECEMBER 1

The centurion said in reply,
"Lord, I am not worthy to have you enter under my roof;
only say the word and my servant will be healed."
—MATTHEW 8:8

The centurion is proof that it's possible to be completely
humble before God while, at the same time, trust God
completely. I can recognize that God is God and I am not.
But that recognition should free me to turn to God with a
receptive, hopeful heart. I can see myself as unworthy and
yet—absolutely loved.

Isaiah 4:2–6
Psalm 122:1–2,3–4b,4cd–5,6–7,8–9
Matthew 8:5–11

DECEMBER 2

Jesus rejoiced in the Holy Spirit and said,
"I give you praise, Father, Lord of heaven and earth,
for although you have hidden these things
from the wise and the learned
you have revealed them to the childlike."
—LUKE 10:21

Because the Scriptures consistently praise wisdom, we know
that Jesus was not discouraging people from learning and
becoming wise. He was pointing out that truth and
understanding come to anyone who has the trust of a child.
He saw people for whom education had become a stumbling
block, leading to pride that closes a person's mind and heart.
May we temper our learning with openness and humility.

Isaiah 11:1–10
Psalm 72:1–2,7–8,12–13,17
Luke 10:21–24

They all ate and were satisfied.
They picked up the fragments left over—seven baskets full.
—MATTHEW 15:37

These Gospel stories are meant to give us images and phrases
to ponder. How often is *every* person well fed and satisfied?
How often do we have abundant leftovers of *anything*? Jesus
was not dealing with a wealthy population; most of his
listeners were ordinary working people, and quite a few were
officially poor. But when Jesus provides, the whole scene
overflows. It's as if he and the Gospel writers seek to startle
us into faith.

Isaiah 25:6–10a
Psalm 23:1–3a,3b–4,5,6
Matthew 15:29–37

DECEMBER 4

• ST. JOHN DAMASCENE, PRIEST AND DOCTOR OF THE CHURCH •

Trust in the LORD forever!
For the LORD is an eternal Rock.
He humbles those in high places,
and the lofty city he brings down;
He tumbles it to the ground,
levels it with the dust.
It is trampled underfoot by the needy,
by the footsteps of the poor.
—ISAIAH 26:4–6

It's impossible to escape this fact: God notices the world's great imbalance between the rich and poor, the high and low. This shows up in Mary's Magnificat and in Jesus' sermons. If I am to follow Jesus on the holy way, I cannot ignore the world's injustice—even if I'd like to pretend the Scriptures don't address it.

Isaiah 26:1–6
Psalm 118:1 and 8–9,19–21,25–27a
Matthew 7:21,24–27

DECEMBER 5

All who are alert to do evil will be cut off,
those whose mere word condemns a man,
Who ensnare his defender at the gate,
and leave the just man with an empty claim.
—ISAIAH 29:20–21

Sooner or later, evil will be cut off—put away from God's presence and realm. Holy Spirit, please sensitize our spirits so that we are not attracted to any form of evil. Sometimes evil is subtle rather than obvious, especially when we are in conflict with others. May we be motivated by justice and mercy always.

Isaiah 29:17–24
Psalm 27:1,4,13–14
Matthew 9:27–31

Saturday

DECEMBER 6

• ST. NICHOLAS, BISHOP •

At the sight of the crowds, his heart was moved with pity for them
because they were troubled and abandoned,
like sheep without a shepherd.
—MATTHEW 9:36

If only we would remember that Jesus always sees us first as
people in need. He does not see screwups and sinners. He
sees those who suffer, who are lost, who need help. When he
looks at you, no matter what kind of day you're having, he is
searching for your need, not your guilt.

Sunday

DECEMBER 7

• SECOND SUNDAY OF ADVENT •

Then the wolf shall be a guest of the lamb,
and the leopard shall lie down with the kid;
the calf and the young lion shall browse together,
with a little child to guide them.

—ISAIAH 11:6

I click on happy animal videos that show up in my social
media feeds. You know the ones: the horse and dog who are
inseparable, the grown lion who remembers the men who
rescued him and tackles them with big-cat hugs. Something
in my heart recognizes a time yet to come, a vision of life
and not death, of collaboration and not predation. Despite
everything that suggests otherwise, I do believe that this
new, bright world is on its way.

Isaiah 11:1–10
Psalm 72:1–2,7–8,12–13,17
Romans 15:4–9
Matthew 3:1–12

• THE IMMACULATE CONCEPTION OF THE BLESSED VIRGIN MARY
(PATRONAL FEAST DAY OF THE UNITED STATES OF AMERICA) •

"Behold, you will conceive in your womb and bear a son,
and you shall name him Jesus.
He will be great and will be called Son of the Most High,
and the Lord God will give him the throne of David his father,
and he will rule over the house of Jacob forever,
and of his Kingdom there will be no end."
—LUKE 1:31–33

How did Mary react after the angel left and his words had time to sink in? It's not like she could share this with her friends and neighbors. Setting aside the impossible pregnancy, any poor country girl who spoke of becoming mother to a future king would be asking for trouble. Mary needed to hold these words closely, meditate on them privately, and proceed with care. Sometimes God plants a future within us that is too disturbing for others to believe or accept. So we wait. And pray.

Genesis 3:9–15,20
Psalm 98:1,2–3ab,3cd–4
Ephesians 1:3–6,11–12
Luke 1:26–38

Tuesday

DECEMBER 9

• ST. JUAN DIEGO CUAUHTLATOATZIN, HERMIT •

"It is not the will of your heavenly Father
that one of these little ones be lost."
—MATTHEW 18:14

I think Jesus understood how quickly people collapse under guilt and wither under shame. He knew that the enemy, called the Accuser, is intent on pushing us away from God by convincing us that God is out for payback, revenge, our humiliation and failure. Some days it's really hard to do, but hang on to Jesus' proclamation here in Matthew 18. Know that God wants you to find your way.

Isaiah 40:1–11
Psalm 96:1–2,3 and 10ac,11–12,13
Matthew 18:12–14

DECEMBER 10

• OUR LADY OF LORETO •

The LORD is the eternal God,
creator of the ends of the earth.
He does not faint nor grow weary,
and his knowledge is beyond scrutiny.
He gives strength to the fainting;
for the weak he makes vigor abound.
—ISAIAH 40:28–29

Try beginning your day by reviewing these truths. God who loves me is the beginning point of everything. And everything about God just keeps being and doing. God is my source, period. And this source is limitless. This is what Jesus invites us to be part of.

Isaiah 40:25–31
Psalm 103:1–2,3–4,8 and 10
Matthew 11:28–30

I am the LORD, your God,
who grasp your right hand;
It is I who say to you, "Fear not,
I will help you."
—ISAIAH 41:13

Those of us fortunate enough to have grown up with at least one loving parent or caregiver can remember the sensation of someone big and safe holding our hand when we were little. There's nothing like the steadiness and security of that firm but tender grasp. In Isaiah's words, God encourages us to think of God as a loving father or mother.

Isaiah 41:13–20
Psalm 145:1 and 9,10–11,12–13ab
Matthew 11:11–15

See, I am coming to dwell among you, says the LORD.
—ZECHARIAH 2:14

Gods should stay far away, above and beyond us, shouldn't they? Aren't we the ones who must find our way out of this life and into the realm of the holy? Isn't that what sacrifices and trials are for? Isn't that why we are told to be good, to do better? Well, no. God, the holy, the only, the eternal, did in fact dwell among us in the person of Jesus. That's not the end of it, either. God continues to dwell among us, with us, in us. We don't have to travel anywhere or solve a grand riddle.

Zechariah 2:14–17 or Revelation 11:19a; 12:1–6a,10ab
Judith 13:18bcde,19
Luke 1:26–38 or 1:39–47
Or any readings from the Common of the Blessed Virgin Mary.

DECEMBER 13

• ST. LUCY, VIRGIN AND MARTYR •

In those days,
like a fire there appeared the prophet Elijah
whose words were as a flaming furnace.
—SIRACH 48:1

Have words ever started a fire in you? You were listening to a speaker or reading a book or happened upon wild words in a movie or on social media. When that happens, pay attention. There's a reason those words sparked a reaction within you.

Sirach 48:1–4,9–11
Psalm 80:2ac and 3b,15–16,18–19
Matthew 17:9a,10–13

DECEMBER 14

• THIRD SUNDAY OF ADVENT •

Take as an example of hardship and patience, brothers and sisters,
the prophets who spoke in the name of the Lord.
—JAMES 5:10

Hardship and *patience*. Those are old-fashioned words, aren't
they? My grandmother used those words. My generation
shied away from them. We thought that everything in life
should go well and that all pain should be short-lived. Then
those of us who became followers of Jesus had to learn the
truth. A faithful, holy, fruitful life will, by its nature, require
hardship and patience. I now consider them aspects of a
healthy "normal."

Isaiah 35:1–6a,10
Psalm 146:6–7,8–9,9–10
James 5:7–10
Matthew 11:2–11

I see him, though not now;
I behold him, though not near:
A star shall advance from Jacob,
and a staff shall rise from Israel.
—NUMBERS 24:17

Those of the ancient world who hoped in God understood
that they would not live to see many of God's wonders
among humanity. Yet they claimed the experience as their
own, simply because they'd been given a vision of it. As I
grow older, I need to let go of this need to experience
everything for myself. I hope in God's wonders that will
occur in the next generation, and the next.

Numbers 24:2–7,15–17a
Psalm 25:4–5ab,6 and 7bc,8–9
Matthew 21:23–27

Tuesday

DECEMBER 16

[Jesus said,] "When John came to you in the way of righteousness,
you did not believe him;
but tax collectors and prostitutes did.
Yet even when you saw that,
you did not later change your minds and believe him."
—MATTHEW 21:32

It's a proud person who remains unmoved at the evidence of
another's changed life. It's a hard heart that dismisses the
transformation in others rather than pays attention to grace
in action. Jesus called this out among those who refused to
believe him. Lord Jesus, open my eyes and my heart to the
wonders you are working in people I see and know.

Zephaniah 3:1–2,9–13
Psalm 34:2–3,6–7,17–18,19 and 23
Matthew 21:28–32

Wednesday

DECEMBER 17

In him shall all the tribes of the earth be blessed;
all the nations shall proclaim his happiness.
—PSALM 72:17

I've lost track of how many times the Scriptures state clearly
that God's mercy and blessing and guidance were always
meant for the whole world, for every nation and people.
Quite amazing how humans become so focused on their own
groups and countries and parties. We Christians are as
inclined as anyone to be narrow-minded and short-sighted.
God, forgive us for neglecting your desires.

Genesis 49:2,8–10
Psalm 72:1–2,3–4ab,7–8,17
Matthew 1:1–17

DECEMBER 18

O God, with your judgment endow the king,
and with your justice, the king's son;
He shall govern your people with justice
and your afflicted ones with judgment.

—PSALM 72:2

I'm not good at remembering to pray for presidents, prime ministers, kings, queens, and congresspeople. But why wouldn't we pray for the people who hold so much influence in the world? This should probably be a goal for the coming year.

Jeremiah 23:5–8
Psalm 72:1–2,12–13,18–19
Matthew 1:18–25

DECEMBER 19

The woman went and told her husband,
"A man of God came to me;
he had the appearance of an angel of God, terrible indeed.
I did not ask him where he came from,
nor did he tell me his name.
But he said to me,
'You will be with child and will bear a son.'"
—JUDGES 13:6–7

The "man of God" appeared first to the woman; eventually he appeared to both wife and husband, and they realized that they were speaking to God's messenger. It's a rather touching story of the Divine interacting with a couple, both of whom respond and do as instructed even though they are somewhat fearful and full of questions. We don't always face spiritual challenges on our own, and this story is a nice reminder of that.

Judges 13:2–7,24–25a
Psalm 71:3–4a,5–6ab,16–17
Luke 1:5–25

DECEMBER 20

Mary said, "Behold, I am the handmaid of the Lord.
May it be done to me according to your word."
Then the angel departed from her.
—LUKE 1:38

I would love to see this event from Gabriel's perspective. We know that Mary said, "Yes, I'll do this." So Gabriel left, no doubt wondering how God of the Universe could entrust such a tremendous task to a frail human, and a girl at that—a young girl with no real power or voice in the world. Was the archangel perplexed? Doubtful that this could really work? Would you or I have chosen such a strategy to mend the world?

Isaiah 7:10–14
Psalm 24:1–2,3–4ab,5–6
Luke 1:26–38

Sunday

DECEMBER 21

[The angel said to Joseph,]
"She will bear a son and you are to name him Jesus,
because he will save his people from their sins."
—MATTHEW 1:21

At least God gave Mary and Joseph a heads-up. Both of them
were informed that their son would have a holy calling. I
wonder how they carried this information through Jesus'
years at home? You wouldn't tell a five-year-old (or even a
fifteen-year-old) that, by the way, he's the messiah. God
counted on Joseph and Mary to handle the situation wisely
and patiently. What a risk to take with human beings. Yet
God takes risks with us all the time.

Isaiah 7:10–14
Psalm 24:1–2,3–4,5–6 (7c,10b)
Romans 1:1–7
Matthew 1:18–24

*Mary remained with Elizabeth about three months
and then returned to her home.*
—LUKE 1:56

Please remember that given this bit of information in Luke,
we know that Mary returned home three months pregnant.
Already showing. I can't imagine the courage it took. No
wonder she stayed with Elizabeth, an older woman who
could set an example of faith and encourage the younger
woman to keep trusting God. The Lord knew that these two
needed each other. Don't be surprised when God sends you
good company while you're trying to follow your calling.

1 Samuel 1:24–28
1 Samuel 2:1,4–5,6–7,8abcd
Luke 1:46–56

DECEMBER 23

• ST. JOHN OF KANTY, PRIEST •

Then fear came upon all their neighbors,
and these matters were discussed
throughout the hill country of Judea.
—LUKE 1:65

All the neighbors were afraid because Elizabeth miraculously
conceived and had a child. You can't keep many secrets in a
tight-knit community. Word gets around that the impossible
has happened, that someone had a vision or an angelic visit,
and normal life has been upended. This makes me wonder,
Am I willing to live a life so touched by God that it's
disturbing to the neighbors?

Malachi 3:1–4,23–24
Psalm 25:4–5ab,8–9,10 and 14
Luke 1:57–66

Wednesday

DECEMBER 24

The LORD also reveals to you
that he will establish a house for you.
And when your time comes and you rest with your ancestors,
I will raise up your heir after you, sprung from your loins,
and I will make his Kingdom firm.
—2 SAMUEL 7:11–12

The story of humanity's salvation is also the story of
belonging and stability. God's love and providence maintain
a through-line in history and across generations. It's good to
remember this when the evening news is terrifying and daily
troubles threaten to overwhelm us.

2 Samuel 7:1–5,8b–12,14a,16
Psalm 89:2–3,4–5,27 and 29
Luke 1:67–79

⇒ 389 ∈

DECEMBER 25

• THE NATIVITY OF THE LORD (CHRISTMAS) •

They shall be called the holy people,
the redeemed of the LORD,
and you shall be called "Frequented,"
a city that is not forsaken.
—ISAIAH 62:12

How's this for an identity: holy person, one of God's family?
How can you live into this identity with more gratitude and
excitement in the weeks and months to come?

VIGIL:
Isaiah 62:1–5
Psalm 89:4–5,16–17,27,29 (2a)
Acts 13:16–17,22–25
Matthew 1:1–25 or 1:18–25

DAWN:
Isaiah 62:11–12
Psalm 97:1,6,11–12
Titus 3:4–7
Luke 2:15–20

NIGHT:
Isaiah 9:1–6
Psalm 96:1–2,2–3,11–12,13
Titus 2:11–14
Luke 2:1–14

DAY:
Isaiah 52:7–10
Psalm 98:1,2–3,3–4,5–6 (3c)
Hebrews 1:1–6
John 1:1–18 or 1:1–5,9–14

*The witnesses laid down their cloaks
at the feet of a young man named Saul.
As they were stoning Stephen, he called out,
"Lord Jesus, receive my spirit."*
—ACTS 7:58–59

The stoning of Stephen begins an era in the early Jesus community. He is the first martyr, and one of those complicit in his death will become a major witness to the Christ not many years from this event. Each of us belongs to a story constantly unfolding. Every event takes its place in the grand drama, and every person is important to the whole. Lord Jesus, help each of us appreciate that we are part of your salvation saga.

Acts 6:8–10; 7:54–59
Psalm 31:3cd–4,6 and 8ab,16bc and 17
Matthew 10:17–22

Saturday

DECEMBER 27

• ST. JOHN, APOSTLE AND EVANGELIST •

We have seen it and testify to it
and proclaim to you the eternal life
that was with the Father and was made visible to us—
what we have seen and heard
we proclaim now to you,
so that you too may have fellowship with us.
—1 JOHN 1:3

I think testimony carried more weight in earlier times than it does now. Nowadays, we must have surveys and statistics and a portfolio and who knows what else before we rely on information. If we're not careful, we will cut ourselves off from community and testimony and flail around with only data and our limited judgment.

1 John 1:1–4
Psalm 97:1–2,5–6,11–12
John 20:1a and 2–8

Sunday

DECEMBER 28

• THE HOLY FAMILY OF JESUS, MARY, AND JOSEPH •

When the magi had departed, behold,
the angel of the Lord appeared to Joseph in a dream and said,
"Rise, take the child and his mother, flee to Egypt,
and stay there until I tell you."
—MATTHEW 2:13

By now, Joseph is used to paying attention to his dreams. Perhaps he's gained help from dreams since he was a youngster, and God knew that a dream was the best way to get Joseph's attention. Here again, a dream provides Joseph with a next step. We admire Joseph for many reasons, but certainly for this one: he was attentive enough to his interior life to recognize God's movement within him.

Sirach 3:2–6,12–14
Psalm 128:1–2,3,4–5
Colossians 3:12–21 or 3:12–17
Matthew 2:13–15,19–23

Monday

DECEMBER 29

• ST. THOMAS BECKET, BISHOP AND MARTYR •

Beloved, I am writing no new commandment to you
but an old commandment that you had from the beginning.
The old commandment is the word that you have heard.
—1 JOHN 2:7

We need not look for new information. There's no magic
formula or secret path we must discover. God has given us
what we need. We already know what we need to know.
Now in my elder years, when I face a dilemma, I don't look
for a new revelation but try to remember what the Holy
Spirit has already taught me. Yes, we can be that confident.

1 John 2:3–11
Psalm 96:1–2a,2b–3,5b–6
Luke 2:22–35

DECEMBER 30

When they had fulfilled all the prescriptions
of the law of the Lord,
they returned to Galilee,
to their own town of Nazareth.
—LUKE 2:39

After the dreams and holy encounters, the gifts of the Magi and the confirmations of elders. After the dramatic pregnancy and precarious birth. After stars and journeys and wonders, Mary, Joseph, and their infant son went home. The task before them was daily life, and it would be many years before the prophecies they'd heard would take shape in any recognizable way. Isn't this the way for all of us? We simply face today, and then tomorrow, and wait for God to create our future.

1 John 2:12–17
Psalm 96:7–8a,8b–9,10
Luke 2:36–40

No one has ever seen God.
The only-begotten Son, God, who is at the Father's side,
has revealed him.
—JOHN 1:18

I encourage you, reader and fellow faith pilgrim, to resist the distractions of argument or even doctrine but to focus on Jesus, who reveals to us what our souls hunger to know about God. Make this your quest for 2026.

1 John 2:18–21
Psalm 96:1–2,11–12,13
John 1:1–18